How to be a Favourite with YOUR BOSS

Discover how sincerity and hard-work always pay in your career

Don Aslet

PUSTAK MAHAL®
Delhi • Bangalore • Mumbai • Patna • Hyderabad • London

This edition has been published in India
by arrangement with **Marsh Creek Press, U.S.A.**

© *Copyright in India by*
Pustak Mahal®, Delhi

J-3/16, Daryaganj, New Delhi-110002
☎ 23276539, 23272783, 23272784 • *Fax:* 011-23260518
E-mail: info@pustakmahal.com • *Website:* www.pustakmahal.com

London Office
5, Roddell Court, Bath Road, Slough SL3 OQJ, England
E-mail: pustakmahaluk@pustakmahal.com

Sales Centre
10-B, Netaji Subhash Marg, Daryaganj, New Delhi-110002
☎ 23268292, 23268293, 23279900 • *Fax:* 011-23280567
E-mail: rapidexdelhi@indiatimes.com

Branch Offices
Bangalore: ☎ 22234025
E-mail: pmblr@sancharnet.in • pustak@sancharnet.in
Mumbai: ☎ 22010941
E-mail: rapidex@bom5.vsnl.net.in
Patna: ☎ 3294193 • *Telefax:* 0612-2302719
E-mail: rapidexptn@rediffmail.com
Hyderabad: *Telefax:* 040-24737290
E-mail: pustakmahalhyd@yahoo.co.in

ISBN 978-81-223-0052-9

Table of Contents

Gender Mender

Bosses come in two sexes. Rather than waste your time and our type with a "he or she" at every reference, we've just equally mixed the usage all through the book.

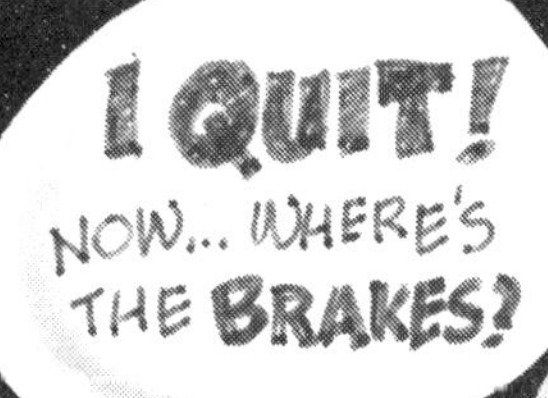

Preface

There is no such thing as a temporary job.

If you're thinking about getting or keeping a job "just to get by" until something better comes along, remember, no job is temporary. Whether you do it for five minutes, five hours, or five years, it is and will be a part of your life. It engraves habits and attitudes into your being, and habits and attitudes aren't temporary, they remain and transfer everywhere with you to bless or curse you. Any activity you engage in for any length of time makes or takes character from you, adds or subtracts commitment, ambition, feelings, and growth. You keep **every-thing** from every job you take. You don't put your life or abilities on hold for a while to work at something until you land that dream job someday.

You can't get back even one minute of time any job consumes. Every job puts its brand on you, and whether you like or love a job or not, it's part of you forever.

So no matter when or where or what or for how long you take a job, make sure you do it the best you can, with all your heart, might, mind, and strength. Because the bottom line is that it really has nothing to do with the nature of the job or the pay or who you're working for—only with your personal effort to give and become your best. The ultimate in life isn't what you do or get, *it's what you become*. No job is temporary, they are all eternal in the sense of effect. So never think of or treat one lightly, because from any job you'll get a pattern, a rhythm, a satisfaction that will never leave you. *All* is the only way to do it.

There is no such thing as a temporary job.

SHIP RULES:
ROW, ROW,
ROW DA BOAT!

Chapter 1

Why Please and Impress the Boss?

There are at least 10,000 possible influences on whether you have a full, happy life or not, but if you boil it down, there are really just a few biggies:

1. Who you marry or choose as a companion
2. Your health
3. Your code of ethics
4. Your job/career

If all four of these are right for you, things can be pretty bright. But if any one of them is in discord, it can throw a real shadow on the other three. You can be madly in love with the best person in the world, have impeccable health, and an enjoyable, high-paying job, but if your ethics are in conflict and confusion it will eventually erode if not destroy the other three. We all know people, on the other hand, who have their ethics in "Scout's honor" order, have a great job, and haven't been sick a day in their life—but they get hooked to another person who is a loser and in a matter of months the three good areas are down the drain. We've also known those who have it all when it comes to job, mate, and code of honor, but then for one reason or another lose their health, and it eliminates their career, burdens their loved ones, and even begins to erode their beliefs.

Our focus here is number 4, because just as many if not more of us in this life mate well, feel superb, and live an honest, serving life, but hate what we do for a living... our job... our career... our profession. When you aren't happy with your job it means you aren't happy with what you're doing for 8 or more hours a day. It's only a matter of time before the same bad feelings poison your personal relationships, destroy your physical and mental health, and compromise your conduct.

Job satisfaction, too, has 10,000 ingredients which boil down to just a few biggies:

- What you do
- How well you do it
- Who you do it for (the boss)

The same "all or none" principle applies here. Don't we all know plenty of people who do their job well and love their boss, but hate what they do? You can be sure job failure and personal unhappiness is inevitable.

We know plenty of people likewise who love what they do and love their boss, but are lousy producers. Here, too, job failure and personal unhappiness is inevitable.

And then there are countless people who love what they do and are good at it, but they just can't get along with their bosses. Job failure and personal unhappiness is right around the corner.

You've already decided what you want and like to do, and your degree of training and commitment will determine how well you do it. This book is going to handle the *boss* angle—that whole big important part of your life. I'm going to give you some "Wow" secrets, solutions, and savvy so you'll know all the what, why, when, and hows of winning over your boss. It will even give you the foundation for being a boss someday. So much effort has gone into telling people how to get a job today, in magazines, newspapers, and books, as well as all kinds of seminars, on radio and TV. Everywhere we turn there are models and instructions for the best cut and color of suit to impress the boss, the best way to type and phrase a resume, all the ways of selling and persuading someone to hire you. But little is said about how to keep a job after you land it, how to do a good job after you get it.

The principles are really very simple, and I promise that the recommendations in these pages will not only help you keep the job you have, but help you enjoy it more, and help you get future jobs, too.

You might think, as you read through this book, that much of what I say here sounds hardhearted or petty, and some of it probably is. But the boss, good or bad, right or wrong, holds a real power position in our lives. He or she can be the key to our whole future. And 98% of bosses agree with the points made in these pages. The minute you are made a boss, maybe just tomorrow morning, you'll expect all of this from every single person who works for you.

A job is generally our vehicle to most of life's destinations—we may be the engine, the starter, the fuel, and the driver, but our job (and hence the boss) is the vehicle. And this is one vehicle we really need to keep running smoothly.

A boss can do more for you than any degree you have or will ever earn. And a good boss *wants* to help make you better, see you excel. Good relationships with past and present bosses are some of the best sources of future jobs, too. As business experts note:

"Jobs and promotions that pay well are usually filled before most people find out about the openings. More than 85% of available jobs are not listed in help-wanted classified ads, because the majority of executives now find employment through networking, that is, by knowing someone who knows someone." (And remember that the boss knows everyone and everyone knows the boss!)

We've all seen employees who seem delighted when their boss or company is in trouble or struggling (don't we all have a vengeful corner somewhere in our hearts?). Kind of a "Good, the big shots are brought down" attitude. This is like loving it when you see a hole in the bottom of the ship you're on. Sure, the captain is in trouble and the ship (company) might sink (it'll serve the taskmaster right!). But where does that leave you and the rest of the crew? Hey, man, anytime there's a leak in the old boat of business you work on and the boss or his job is threatened, remember you're on the same ship and you can drown just as easily. So I'd be looking for leaks, reporting leaks, and fixing leaks, even if I didn't give a hoot about the captain.

A good reference

(What your boss can do for you, why break your butt for your boss.)

We'll work and pay four or more years to get a degree, mainly to qualify us for a "good" or "better" job. What if I tell you you could work 4-6 months, get paid for it, and end up with a piece of paper a hundred times more powerful than a diploma? You can! It's called a "reference," and it's not a record of where you worked, or what you did and when. I'm talking about a personally written letter or call from your ex-boss to your potential new boss. Resumes and records tell very little. A real rousing reference is what you need to rocket you past your competitors into a new job or higher pay and position. References are believable. They say what *is*, not what could be, or what you trained or practiced for.

Let me give you a good example. During the 60's my company was still new and growing, toward the Grand Canyon in one direction (yes, national parks need cleaning too), and the beautiful Sun Valley resort in the other. I hired a young woman of twenty by the name of Jeanne McWillis, from a small town in the West. Her husband was a freshman at Idaho State, and she was the sole support of the family. She didn't have a degree, she was just anxious and willing to work. She ran the entire office operation of our cleaning company, so she really had five bosses, and anything could happen anytime, and usually did. She tackled every job with radiance, on the run, and we really appreciated that. We treated her well and paid her well, and when she left we all pitched in to get her the traditional watch. This one was engraved and had a diamond, too, because she truly was a jewel. Her husband had his degree now, and they were moving to Salt Lake City, where he'd be going for his masters, and this fine woman was still his sole support.

One afternoon I got a reference call from a dry cleaner/laundry where she'd applied for a $1.65 an hour (minimum wage) job. I called her immediately and asked her why she was taking this job when she had ten times the ability.

"Jobs are scarce, I mean zero here right now, Don. I don't have a degree to flash so I'm willing to take anything just to work and earn." I asked her what the best job she'd applied for was. Administrative assistant, she said, for a top executive of a national media corporation in a nice office downtown. It paid four times what the laundry did. "I'd never get that job, there's a line of college graduates with qualifications you wouldn't believe." "Give me the phone number," I said. She did, and I called the giant corporation and went through three secretaries to get the head honcho. "Mr. Smith, I'm Don Aslett (I then gave him a two-sentence background on myself). You've had a Jean McWillis apply for the position of administrative assistant? Well

Mr. Smith, if you miss her you'll be passing up one of the best people who's been through your door in the past twenty years. This woman worked for me for four years and did payroll, accounting, PR, collections, typing, errands, cleaning, and thirty other jobs. I'll tell you without hesitation that she can outwork, outproduce, and outclass any five of the best other applicants in line for that job. She is a superwoman, and she'll instill a spirit of wholesomeness and industry into your staff that you won't believe. If you don't hire her you'll be making the biggest mistake of your career."

The guy hired Jeanne within ten minutes of my call, without a degree, test, or additional interview. This is what's called a good reference, and I give these happily to those who deserve them, and like Mr. Smith, I hire from those I get.

Everyone can supply some kind of reference, no big deal, but good references, those where your former boss will truly endorse you, go to bat for you, are unquestionably the biggest single reason to really break your butt for someone. Because I'm a public figure now, and a boss of thousands, I have plenty of people putting my name down as a reference—Scouts from 20 years back, students from 30 years back, etc. For some of these folks I can give some kind of reference like "Yes, they worked for me October 68 to November 74." They were nice guys and their work was satisfactory. I've done at least a thousand of these and they're asleep on the page.

But if you've done a job, a real job, for your boss it counts more than the position or salary you left with. It beats degrees and diplomas and is pure dynamite. It earns you a letter like I wrote not long ago for a young woman leaving because her husband was transferred:

CONTRACTORS, INC.

PO BOX 700 POCATELLO ID 83204 208 232 6212
DON ASLETT, CHAIRMAN OF THE BOARD

November 5, 1991

RE: Letter of Recommendation

For: Virginia Cotter

From: Don A. Aslett

It is a pure privilege to have the opportunity to write a letter of recommendation for someone like Virginia, who could easily be summed up in one word: OUTSTANDING! Virginia is quick, pleasant, can and will pick up any assignment in minutes and do it well. She radiates life and enthusiasm, and is of excellent character. The bottom line is she's a joy to be around. Best of all, Virginia is a super productive person. I would stand in line to hire her. We all groaned and whimpered when we heard she was moving to Twin Falls, for we had great plans for her here. If you need any further information or would like to talk to me personally, please call me at 208-232-6212.

Sincerely,

VARSITY CONTRACTORS, INC.

Don A. Aslett

Don A. Aslett

When she plops that letter down on a prospective boss's desk with my name on it, she's going to be hard to out do with looks or diplomas. A good reference is the best part of a portfolio. It beats money in a savings account. Bosses really believe and depend on other bosses, and references are one way they really help each other—and you—out.

Meet St. Peter here and now

A boss is really sort of a "St. Peter" on earth—in a position to assign, evaluate, approve, reject, or reward. They can let us in or keep us out.

We don't have the option of liking or disliking our boss—we either work with them or against them. We may think:

"I don't have to like the boss, as long as I do my job well." WRONG!

I laughed the first time I heard the Golden Rule of business: "He with the gold rules." Right or wrong, fair or not, this is the way it is. If we work under them, if we want to survive and prosper, our only real option is to obey them. We hear constant discussion about job security through tenure, unions, family ties, etc. These may offer some security, but nothing compared to being liked or respected by the boss.

Our boss unquestionably has more influence on our nest egg than any banker or broker.

And whether we like it or not, the boss is the "receptacle" for the "electric current" of all our work efforts and our career. If things get unplugged or shorted out we never reach our top potential. If we have a good, firm, clear connection, on the other hand, we'll live to carry some real *power* in our job position, present and future.

How do I really Rate with the Boss?

After you answer the following, compute your score by giving yourself a 1 for each "Never," a 2 for each "Sometimes," etc., then add up the totals of all the columns.

	Never 1	Sometimes 2	At Least Half the Time 3	Most of the Time 4	Always 5
1. I am punctual (on time) with my work and my projects					
2. I am clean, neat, and organized					
3. I am a peacemaker					
4. When I'm working, I give it all I've got					
5. I am in good health and physical condition					
6. I am honest					
7. I am a team person					

8. My criticisms are polite and constructive					
9. I refrain from second-guessing the boss					
10. I don't carry nuisance habits (gum chewing, smoking, nonstop coffee or cola sipping, etc.) to work with me					
11. I am ambitious and eager					
12. I am flexible and adaptable to change					
13. I am courteous to customers and co-workers					
14. My language is free of profanity and vulgarity					
15. I practice and study to improve my work skills					
16. I volunteer					
17. I control my mood swings					
18. I am loyal to my boss and the company					
TOTAL EACH COLUMN	+	+	+	+	
GRAND TOTAL					

18-36—Pardon me, but your pink slip is showing.	**37-54**—You're nearing the danger zone.	**55-72**—Things are probably okay for now.	**73-90**—You must be on the boss's "Most Wanted" list.

MR. WIPPETT
BIG KAHUNA

Chapter 2

"De-Mything" the Boss

Something's different today. You got up two hours earlier than usual, jotted down notes and plans, placed a few calls, and then made it to the office far ahead of the workpack. Before anyone else even arrived, five calls came in for you: 1. The police called to report that a back door of the building was left open last night. 2. One of your janitors forgot to empty Ms. Important's wastebasket yesterday, and the head of the company she works for called to let you know about it. 3. Your receptionist called in, her baby son bumped his shins so she won't be in today. 4. The Boy Scouts called to remind you of your promised appearance in the upcoming variety show. 5. Your wife called to tell you UPS delivered the new computer component to your house instead of the office.

It's still not 8:00 a.m. yet, and the mail that was just brought in makes it clear that a key client didn't make his payment when he said he would, so you won't have the money you were counting on in time to cover tomorrow's payroll. (Ah well, you've gone without your own check before, and you can do it now, to make sure everyone else gets paid.) You're right in the middle of settling a dispute between two departments over some shared storage space, when your secretary tells you two more callers are waiting: an employee looking for a reference and a supply salesman. (It's still not 9:00.) As soon as the salesman leaves, she informs you that the drum on the $5500 copier is gone already. A new copier is $7500, a used one we'll have to find out how much, and a new drum $600. (There goes your vacation money.) By the end of the morning you've answered eight calls and done the follow-up work they made necessary, given two donations, and turned down two other requests for the same (to people who now hate you). Your secretary reminds you that the second remodeling job to accommodate the company's expansion is underway, and a detailed diagram of all work stations, complete with an inventory and measurements of all furnishings, is needed by Wednesday (three days' work, and one day to do it in). "And don't forget, the fire marshal is coming on Friday."

At noon you head off to give a speech to the local business luncheon. You have to do so much talking both during and after your speech that there's no time to eat. You've been running a fever and now feel mighty queasy, but going home isn't an option—people are counting on you and waiting for you, and you don't get sick leave. So you just go to the restroom and throw up quietly and keep on going.

Now you sit in on a safety meeting called by your insurance company, which informs you that 36 of your last 50 employee Worker's Compensation claims are known to be fraudulent, but caving in and paying is cheaper than paying lawyers $100 an hour to fight. As you leave the meeting one of your staff hands you a proposal for upgrading the phone system (everyone in the office wants it) that would cost $13,000 to implement (you just put in "the best" two years ago).

Now you learn that two good people have put in for the receptionist's job that's open, and their qualifications are so close that personnel didn't dare decide, they left it up to you to do so—today, please.

In between six more calls, all requiring a business decision of some kind, one of your people calls to inform you that they're moving to a new apartment. Can they borrow the company's (your) nice big truck? You say yes, even though you know the tank is full now but when the truck comes back tomorrow it'll only be a quarter full. As your son calls to remind you of his soccer game tonight, you notice the place is empty because it's now 5:00 p.m. You stay to catch up on some things, timing your arrival home to coincide with supper.

The minute you walk through the door, your family presents a schedule for the evening nearly equal to the one at work today. You get the usual average of two work calls at home tonight, one at 8:30 and one at 9:45. You go to bed at 11:00, and flip through a professional journal till you fall asleep at midnight. You need some sleep because tomorrow, believe it or not, is going to be a lot busier.

What was different?

You were the boss today!

The day described above might sound extreme but it's close to average. I've seen days as a boss with double this kind of action. Bosship is by no means all neat stuff and lording-it-over opportunities. If they traded places for a day the average employee would be devastated and the boss would think he had the day off. The bottom line is that the boss is exactly like you, he or she just has a lot more to do and a lot more things to worry about.

TV, movies, cartoons, and colorful exaggerations over the years have ballooned the boss into a beast instead of the buddy he or she really is. We see the trail boss shoot any cowboy who crosses him, or Captain Bligh give a thousand lashes to anyone who polishes the deck poorly.

In most people's minds the word "boss" is equivalent to ogre, a real heavy, someone who doesn't do anything but sneak around and snoop, who loves to make employees squirm, and looks hard all day for reasons to fire you. The boss gets rich exploiting us and doesn't know a thing about what's actually going on.

We come to the workplace all prepared for a Dagwood and Mr. Dithers relationship.

Almost the total opposite is true on every count. Many people have never really met or gotten acquainted with the boss, only his silhouette or shadow, which is often a creation of paranoid imagination.

The idea that bosses are "Scrooges" who plan all year to work you until midnight on Christmas Eve, or the image of the old bent wizened storekeeper who counts and re-counts the pennies in the register after you leave, is nowhere close to the truth. I've hardly ever had or met a boss like this. Most are more compassionate than many in their workforce. That's why they **are** a boss most of the time—because they know and love people, the company, and it's mission.

After many employees get to really know the boss, they say "Wow, he sure changed!" Not so, you did! You've finally discovered that the boss is a real person with feelings, problems, and longings just like you.

YOU are a boss's diamond asset. YOU save his job, YOU make him look good, YOU make him money, YOU get him raises. The boss has no reason in the world to want to do anything to you except help and bless you. A boss is nothing without you, and if you "go" for any reason, good or bad, it reflects badly upon them. They get questioned, they have to do your work, and they have to replace you, which is hard work.

Ninety percent of the bosses you'll have in your career will:

- Pay you before themselves
- Look for opportunities to pay you more
- Worry about you more than they worry about themselves
- Work 20 or 30 hours a week more than you
- Know how to do your job better than you
- Have a lot more to lose than you do

I know there are exceptions, there are some real bad bosses out there. (And I wouldn't work for them, see Chapter 5). There are a few people around who see a boss position as a chance to exercise vanity rather than a heightened sense of responsibility, who see promotion as some kind of automatic elevation. But even with superiors like this it's possible to let childish pompousness pass and deal with the position itself respectfully. Showing respect for rank doesn't demean us or mean mindless submission, and observing protocol does help keep things smooth and orderly.

In my college days when I was in ROTC and the National Guard, I was a lowly private. I knew what a sergeant was, with those three gleaming stripes, but I never made any real effort to learn all of the hollowed ranks above that. At summer training camp one day as I came bounding out of the barracks I passed a guy in fatigues. "Hi, buddy," I said, whisking by. "Just a minute, soldier," came an icy reply, "do you know what this is?" he said, pointing to a little black feather-duster-like pin on his collar. "Nope." I said.

"This says I'm a colonel, soldier." At that moment, although he was a lot smaller and maybe not as strong as me and dressed no better, he was the big boss. And in the military it's good manners and a real butt saver to salute your boss. I snapped to attention and saluted smartly, and he smiled kindly and saluted back and said "That's much better, soldier." You can bet my eyeballs did long-range collar darting after that, and I learned all the ranks and enjoyed paying salute respect to my superiors, and enjoyed their salutes back. It didn't mean I was inferior, or that they were bigger or better than me, but they had earned their rank and it deserved acknowledgment.

Today I often work for and around people half my age, who have half my education that I could buy and sell in a minute. But when they are in charge—my boss—I snap to, and say Sir and Ma'am and follow orders. And whether they're a good colonel or a bad colonel, they **are** "the colonel."

Some of you have been or will be surprised to find out that your boss is slower, dumber, older, or younger than you. Or undeserving, or a man when you expected a woman, or vice versa, or even all of the above. But bosshood isn't based on any of the above, and note that bosses aren't called "Your Honor" or "Your Eminence." They, like you, worthy or not, have a certain position and certain responsibilities—in their case they've been chosen or assigned "captain." Your job is to follow them, not nit-pick or get obsessed with every minor injustice. Bosses are human, too, entirely capable of wheel-spinning or sinning.

The boss isn't anxious to fire you

You hold the boss's job in your hands—yes you do! A boss is nobody without us to direct, assign, and schedule. If we get discouraged, go sour, quit, fail, or leave, then the boss suffers—bad. We get this backwards too often, we think bosses are just itching to fire us, that they live to catch us fouling up or arriving late, etc., so they can pounce on us and make us miserable. Most people think it's the boss's whole purpose to beat and CIA us into submission. But bosses hate to fire people, it kills them to fire people. It's the bitterest, most unpleasant thing they ever do, hundreds of times worse than going to the dentist. When you stay and do well, it's the boss's delight. When you fail and go, it's nothing but trouble. Have you ever thought what a boss goes through when they lose a member of the crew or staff?

1. First, depending on the position, it costs hundreds or even thousands of dollars to refill it, assuming it can be refilled.
2. The team suffers (or falls apart) and production is lost, while a replacement is sought.
3. The boss's boss loses some faith in, and respect for, the boss.

4. It hurts the boss's leadership of other employees.
5. It always causes ripples of talk and gossip (and loss of production) in the whole staff/crew.
6. Many pages of paperwork (forms, payroll reports, etc.) have to be done.
7. It's a nightmare for accounting—new files, entries, etc.
8. The boss has to retrain and reintroduce the new person to everything.
9. Customers and clients have to adjust to a new face and personality (and they hate it).
10. All in all, it takes many hours of the boss's time just to get back to where they were.

With all these headaches to look forward to, why would a boss ever want to fire you or make you contemplate leaving? When you do well and stay, the boss looks good, really good. They love it. Bosses dread firing or turnover more than any other part of their job. So relax and work really hard!

You'll be secure and the boss will itch to help you advance yourself and get raises. That's what they really want because when you are riding high, they are riding higher. They'll love you for it, will protect you, and spend their time trying to make you happy.

Does the boss actually do anything?

Many times, in your years of work, it will appear that you are doing all the work, while the boss is doing little (or none). Yet he is getting twice or three times the pay you are, which hardly seems fair. This is a false perception, as most bosses will tell you. Or you will find it out, when you move up in your job.

Twenty years ago, when $200,000 was still a lot of money, a group of us were discussing a business acquaintance whose annual salary had just reached that lofty amount. He'd been promoted to division president by his company, a large chemical manufacturing conglomerate. All of us were earning much less, and we were conjecturing what it would be like to be in that heady compensation range. One of the guys said, "Wow! $200,000 a year. That's almost $100 an hour for an average workday. Why, it costs them a hundred bucks just to have the guy eat lunch! What could he possibly do, hour after hour, day in and day out, to make him worth $100 an hour?" (This was back in the days when $100 was a healthy car payment, and $250 per month would buy a nice house.)

Another of the businessmen present made a very astute observation. He said: "He probably doesn't do something each and every hour to make him worth $100. About once a week, though, or maybe only twice a month, he'll be called upon to make a decision which has the potential to impact his company to the tune of hundreds of thousands, or even millions of dollars. If he can make good decisions consistently, that's what makes him worth the $200,000 per year. There are probably many decisions he makes a year where each one alone would be worth more than his yearly salary."

I was impressed with that reasoning, and have thought since how easy it is to misjudge things like this. You might observe this manager engaged in some of the more mundane duties of his office, or just relaxing in order to bring his mind to sharp focus, and think he doesn't do much to earn that salary. Right at that moment, though, he may have been formulating a plan of action or reaching a key decision which would move the division forward in a major way, protecting everyone's livelihood and strengthening their earning ability.

Lots of bosses are longing to be back in the rank and file line, where they wouldn't have the burden of responsibility, the mental anguish, the added hours. When you compare pay, be sure to add in those extra hours. In more than thirty-five years now as a boss, my normal work day is 12 1/2 hours, and I've had many a 14-hour day. Most bosses I know, counting the company work they do at home and early and late, average at least ten-hour days. And most of that, trust me, is tougher than the nice work you get to do. It's things like scheduling, fighting finances, handling problems they didn't cause, cleaning up after people, dealing with the wrath of offended customers and clients, etc. Don't spend too much time worrying about and wanting the boss's job—you might get it and get the surprise of your life.

Bosses aren't rich

Here it is folks, the biggest surprise of all. "In business" doesn't mean bursting with money. Eighty percent (that's eight out of ten!) of businesses fail, go broke, gone, dead! The biggest reason is no money. At the end of the month, bosses go through piles of bills and credit card statements just like you do, except theirs are bigger and there's more bad news in them. After all you have only one or two people charging things, and they have many. Those buildings and bank accounts, fleets of vehicles, and all that equipment you see owned by the company are generally financed and owned by the bank, while your boss is sweating blood to make the payments. In my own case, it took twenty solid years of sacrifice to keep my business going and come up with the capital to keep operating. Four times my own family phone and lights were shut off. I was threatened and sued by creditors and the IRS, and there were times I didn't even have enough money to buy milk or clothes for the kids. All the while most of my employees and the community were convinced I was a millionaire at least, and were jealous of my big company and the luxury they thought I lived in. All because I had a lot of people working for me and owned a "company."

I remember once when I was really down and out, our city Little League came in for a donation. I gave them $150, the last penny I had, and the woman was disgusted. "Well from a person of your wealth we expected seven or eight hundred dollars toward those new uniforms."

Likewise, my oldest daughter went to college on a shoestring. When she got out, she started two women's clothing stores in a nearby mall. The rent was $1700 a month, and she barely scraped by every month for a year, not making any profit but hoping to build sales. She finally closed one store, then the other. In four years she never made any money, but to all her employees (many of whom helped themselves to clothes and shaved their hours), all her friends, and all the local characters who came by each day, she was rich because she had **two** stores.

A CPA told me some surprising stories about a neighborhood inhabited by half bosses and half workers. One couple who owned and ran a business, for example, ended out the year making $28,000, while their neighbors, a man and wife who worked on a staff and crew, made $61,000 (all the while, of course, commenting on how rich the store owners were).

Few bosses are actually richer than you, they're just bigger riskers than you, and are attempting to gain more independence and wealth in the far distant future. Few, darn few, have it now—trust me, I know hundreds of bosses! Expecting a boss to be able to pay your way through life because they are super rich is a super error—it just isn't so!

The boss has bosses, too

Probably the biggest surprise you'll ever have in your life is the big day when you finally get out from under a boss and become a boss yourself. Your troubles and all that kowtowing are now over. What a relief, you're now in charge instead of being charged!

Surprise, surprise, surprise—as a boss you don't have a boss, you now have a whole battery of bosses! Bosshood is definitely not an immunity from answering to authority, a boss has a lot more people to please than anyone who works under him or her ever will.

The first one is a cold-hearted, greedy, unyielding, demanding fellow you've heard about but probably never had much contact with: Uncle Sam. He has at least twenty assistant bosses, too, from the IRS to the Environmental Protection Agency to OSHA, and they all have rules, regulations, recommendations, orders, quotas, reports, inspections, and schedules you now have to worry about.

Right behind Uncle Sam in the line are clients and customers, insurance brokers,

lawyers, bankers, stockholders, partners, and boards of directors, who will all now be telling you what, when, where, and how to do.

Every boss knows well what it's like to have a boss because they have plenty of them. Most of the time this makes your boss pretty understanding of you. There are bosses who remain intimidating jerks or tyrants, but be assured they are suffering more than you. They have to plan and live with the misery they deal out, and they have to face each day not being loved or even liked by workers, family, or friends. That's LONESOME in capital letters!

The boss has a family, too!

We all worry about ourselves and our loved ones so much we often forget others have families, too. At work, for example, we tend to feel it's the company's or boss's job to make us happy and take care of our family, and we forget that our boss or the owner of the company has a family, too.

In fact the main reason most bosses started and are running the place you work is to provide a good life for their own family. Since their underlying purpose is to enhance their family in any way they can, many of them use their business not just for the money it earns, but as a training ground, a place for their spouse, children, relatives, and even friends to make contacts and gain experience. As an employee you'll see times when "family" get breaks and advantages and positions you don't. Before you cry "Unfair!" try to remember the whole reason the business (which provides you, a nonrelative, a job) even exists.

This reminds me of the hired hand who came to his old farmer boss and said, "You know, Ron, your four boys are doing a pretty poor job of taking care of those cows. Get rid of those boys and you'll have better cows." The old farmer turned to the hired man and said, "I'm not raising cows, Hank, I'm raising boys." His "operation" wasn't the heart of his business, his boys were. A boss may well want to put a son or daughter to work in his or her business, to teach them the trade or even just to keep them out of trouble or save them from something else. Again, this is their purpose and privilege, the reason they pay for everything and take all the risks—the #1 reason their business exists. If you feel this is unfair or unjust or somehow imposes on your honor, then don't work for them.

ZZZZZz
ZZZZZZz

Chapter 3

Your Place in the Workplace

I've always loved airplanes. When I was eight, I was at the head of my class in airplane drawing and study of the aerodynamics of flight. By ten, I had a fleet of model planes carved from old barn doors and posts. At fifteen I actually touched the outside of a two-seater Cessna a farm neighbor owned. By the age of twenty-one I flew island to island in Hawaii in a DC-3. It was as sleek and smooth-sailing as all my pictures and models had been. By the age of forty-five, I had ten years of higher education and a million-plus miles clocked in the air, as a passenger. I knew the mechanics and jargon of airplanes and I'd really lucked-out: one of my cleaning company associates, Dave Miller, was a former commercial pilot. He had his own plane now, and on trips back and forth to his Florida branch of our operation, we flew that twin-engined beauty everywhere. He was an errorless pilot and he educated me on everything, let me read the flight maps, check the oil and gas, etc. Flight after flight, he explained all the whats and whys and wheretofores as he sat flying the plane relaxed and effortlessly.

One day as we taxied out on a North Carolina runway, Dave leaned back and said: "How would you like to take her off and fly her?" "Why not?" I knew so much, and had been with him and watched everything for two years now. So I did, and to save my reputation, I'll spare you the gory details of what followed. I'm sure the FAA reported the plane as "intoxicated " or afflicted with Parkinson's disease. I swerved and hopped down the runway, pitched and swayed and rolled as Dave shot out forty rules, laws, tricks, do's, and don'ts I'd never heard before. It was ugly. When I finally got up in the air and thought I was level, I was climbing or diving at record speed. When I was sure I was heading directly west, I was sliding sideways due east. I couldn't understand a word of the control tower talk crackling at me. The plane was quivering and lunging all over—I'd barely touch something and the plane would peel off like a P-51 on a carrier raid. All those gauges I "knew by heart" had to be read and comprehended and calculated now simultaneously, and as distracted as I was struggling with it all, I couldn't even read the clock!

I don't sweat easily, but by now you could

have squeegeed me off! Finally, fearful that the air patrol would pick up his plane for doing aerobatics without a license, Dave took control. And just as a baby hushes at its mother's touch, all became instant velvet. In that moment, for perhaps the first time, I understood clearly the difference between the on-the-job seat and the onlooker's seat. There are hundreds of little, almost too basic to mention rules and skills, and if they're not followed, things just don't go smoothly. I was sincere and determined, but that wasn't enough. Like it or not, the workplace is the driver's seat. So you won't sweat or get fired like I did on my first flight, here are the solid workanotics for a smoother trip on your job.

The basic boss/employee exchange

By the time I was a junior in college, I'd hired hundreds of different people, mostly fellow students. But just when you think you've heard from and hired all kinds, you run across someone truly unique. A student, a senior, for example, came in for a job interview with his wife. He wanted and needed a job badly, and I needed a special person for a special spot. After I'd outlined the job and its above-average pay and decided to give it to him, he and his wife clasped hands in glee. He went to work the next day. Two weeks later, he tapped on my office door and informed me he was quitting.

"Why? It's a great job, with great pay!" I said. "Yes" he answered, "but work takes up all the time on the job." My brow wrinkled as I asked him to run that past me again. "I said the work takes up all the time on the job," he repeated, more slowly this time. "Isn't that what a job is supposed to do?" I asked, still definitely in the dark. "Well, you see my buddy, who's in engineering like me, has a job where all he has to do is read a gauge for five minutes or so every hour and all the rest of the time he can study. I need a job like that. This a good job, but I have to work all the time."

"I see," I said, "in other words you want me, a fellow struggling student, to pay you for your study time." He hung his head and said "Well gosh, I never thought of it quite that way. I didn't figure you were paying, I kind of thought the company paid."

Big surprise! The workplace is *somebody's*, some person's place. Companies, corporations, stores, offices, and shops don't sign paychecks—people do. You work for people, and answer to them. When you take a job, you go to a workplace to earn money to pay for your homespace. You sell your time for a fee (an hourly rate or salary)—you agree to give your time and energy to the boss and the boss agrees to pay you an agreed-upon amount for it. You're partners: You owe the boss the work and he or she owes you the pay. The violation of this simple exchange won't just ruin your day—it can ruin jobs, companies, and lives when there isn't fairness and honesty at both ends.

When I worked at the Sun Valley Resort in Idaho, I had night crews and my supervisor Frank was supposed to keep them staffed, inspect their work, help them when necessary, and do get-ahead work as needed. He was getting $3.50 an hour (great pay in those days) for this. After a few weeks on the job, Frank found an attic where the extra Beautyrests were stored, and after getting the crews underway, he'd shuffle off the scene and sack out for a couple of hours, and then show back up at the end of the shift to check up and chew out. It never takes long for someone to be willing to fink on their buddies, so before you know it Frank was caught and confronted. "Sure I do," he said when I asked him about it—he saw nothing wrong with it, even if there were parts of his job not getting done. So I tried putting it in the simplest possible terms: "I'm paying you $3.50 an hour for 8 hours of work. If you sleep 2 hours of it, you've ripped me off for $7.00, exactly the same as if you broke into my home or office and stole $7.00 out of the drawer. Slacking or taking time to do personal things on the job, when you're being paid to work is stealing, plain and simple." Frank, who was only 23, understood and agreed. He'd never thought about it that way before.

Doing personal stuff on company time is dishonest.

You're on your honor to keep your end of the bargain, to give your boss the time you agreed to give. Coming in late, leaving early, sleeping, or daydreaming on the job is cheating. Likewise, anytime you extend the agreed-upon or allowed lunch or break time for purely personal reasons you are stealing. And depending on your job, you're costing your boss not only the value of the lost time, but the lost business or opportunities or bad customer relations because you weren't at your post.

Making personal calls, doing personal errands, or reading personal stuff on company time is also dishonest. You're taking the boss's money for time you aren't giving to the job. Ripping off a boss like this really irritates them, and believe me bosses watch and know all of the little techniques and routines for slacking, even the sneakiest ones.

You're sent off somewhere to a seminar or training session, for example, and your boss pays for your travel, food, and lodging as well as your wages and the cost of the session itself. Then when you skip half the sessions to go shopping, you're stealing hundreds of dollars from your boss.

Coffee breaks have come to be interpreted as a God-given right, when actually they are a privilege—you get paid to sit and visit and rest, etc. Stretching breaks like this even a couple of minutes is no different than scooping money out of the cash register.

Giving full measure

or working the whole time on the job

During the time when I had the cleaning and maintenance contract at Sun Valley, I had several young men who did odd jobs for me—landscaping, moving, building demolition, etc. Although in their own minds they were really hot stuff, I had to stay with them constantly to watch, help, and teach them. When the summer ended they went back to school, and to their positions as linemen on the university football team.

Then I hired a gentleman of 62 and amazingly, he managed to take the place of all three of them. He didn't seem to move as fast as the "studs," but the number of jobs accomplished in a month and the profit we made on them sure went up. This fellow's name was Bill Johnson, and I loved working around him. He worked the whole time he was on the job, and his whole secret was just a bunch of little things he did. He always carried his lunch so he wouldn't have to waste an hour driving to and from the cafe. He always showed up with sharp tools and a full chalk line, and he always came equipped with gloves, boots, coat, or hat, whatever the conditions called for, so he wasn't forever shivering or coughing. He didn't talk much, and he always worked while he talked (most people stop to talk). He didn't try to pick and choose jobs to get the easiest one, the lightest end or the cleanest toilet.

And one great, great principle he taught me is that he always showed up early enough

An overall look at the* Boss *or the* Company *we all work for:

They are the reason for our job, they give us the opportunity to earn a living. They ought to be our best friend, and we theirs!

The process is simple. The boss/company buys our time to do things that need done. This often means servicing clients or customers. In the case of professional cleaners, for example, this means not to judge, cuss, or evaluate the customers, but to clean up before and after them. We keep the boss happy by keeping them happy.

Because the boss or the company is buying our time, they're pretty sensitive about how we use it on the job. This is just a principle we're all familiar with—wanting to get what you pay for.

We have a real moral obligation here. It isn't right or honest to take someone's money and then not deliver the time, work and effort we promise in exchange for it.

to get his tools ready, his protective gear on, his hair combed or his pit stop taken care of. The studs always seemed to work hard, but they were only able to get about 6 hours of actual work done in an 8-hour day. About a half hour before the end of the day, for example, they started winding down—finding their coats, putting their tools away. Old Bill, however, worked right up to the official quitting time, and then gathered his tools and packed up his gear on his own time. "I'm not paid to poop around or prepare," he said, "I'm paid to work"—and he did. I've followed this practice ever since with my own "bosses"—my clients—and it's earned me a lot of respect and given me a good feeling about myself.

I've asked platoons of people over the years what an honest day's work is, and the best answer I've ever gotten came from a seventh grader (Lori Burrup of Pocatello, Idaho):

"You feel good about what you did when you go home, and maybe the rest of your life."

Why the boss wants you to be healthy

Not long ago my son-in-law, an executive of one of the country's top companies, informed me that the last five men and women he interviewed for his staff were rejected by the company for poor health. They were young, intelligent, and willing, but through health abuses such as overeating, drinking, and lack of exercise, they'd gotten themselves in such poor physical condition that the company just didn't want them. We're not talking about handicaps here—handicapped people can be some of the best employees ever—but about people who seem to have a constant succession of ailments, largely as a result of their own neglect and self-abuse.

Would you hire a sick person? Probably not. One of a boss's biggest nightmares these days is the ever-rising cost of health insurance. As a result, we bosses now avoid people in ill health like the plague! There are platoons of people out there trying desperately to get with a company that has a good health plan to take care of them, and companies likewise are doing all they can to avoid getting stuck with such people. "Your health is your personal responsibility, not mine," is the boss's true attitude here, and you can't blame them. No business can really afford to budget for everyone's headaches and heartaches. "Sick leave" comes out of the boss's or the company's pocket, not some bank account or

insurance fund somewhere. So bosses, owners, and especially fellow workers can come to dislike you for burdening them.

A boss expects to see you at work EVERY DAY, physically and mentally healthy. Not being there to do your job is by far the biggest reason for lost jobs. Being there **most** days at work isn't enough, you were hired to be there all days.

"Well, I can't help it if I'm sick or injured" is supposed to be an all-forgiving excuse for missing work. But **why** you are gone is not the question/issue in the workplace. It's the simple fact that you aren't there. So there's no one to wait tables, serve customers, sell, drive, type, sing, dance, dig, etc.

"But the flu is going around" really doesn't cut it when customers are lined up at your slot. My doctor tells me that 66% of "sickness" is actually self-induced. **You did it yourself,** somehow. Me and 99% of other bosses (your boss, too) just don't feel sorry for the average self-induced sickness. Particularly from injuries suffered during weekend liesure and recreational activities!

Coming in when you aren't really capable of working isn't much better than being out. I have people show up with pulled ligaments, sunburns, handball bruises, hangovers, etc. from a high-rolling weekend. Then they limp and groan around and spend the best part of the next two days telling all the other workers how this ill fate befell them (while they were playing). It's a real cheat to take someone's money for recuperating on the job.

Healthy people maintain a healthy status with the boss. A "sicko" reputation can be fatal, so stay well. Period. (And don't spread any germs around, either!)

Why the boss wants you to be safe

We all used to laugh at slips on banana peels, sore backs, pulling the chair out from under people when they weren't looking, etc. Those days are gone forever—safety is a big serious subject now. I hold more safety meetings in my company now than any other kind.

There is never a "good place" to get hurt, yet you'll hear workers say in conversation that it's much better to have it happen on the job—then someone else pays for it. That someone else isn't the insurance company, the state, or the federal government, it's your boss—he pays. The responsibility of keeping you from getting hurt on the job is a huge one, because an injury can be a disaster to a family, as well as the company.

If you can convince a boss that you're a safe worker, you'll have an edge over every one of your competitors for that job. These days a good safety record beats a Ph.D., when it comes to hiring. A bad cut or fall doesn't just cost the company, it costs you dearly for the rest of your life. Not only the pain and inconvenience of the injury itself, but the "reckless" or "careless" label it hangs on you. No boss wants unsafe people anymore. Accident insurance used to be an average cost of doing business—now it's a major, major one. If your accident ratio is high, it's a big reason not to hire you, or to get rid of you.

Why the boss wants you to be drug-free

Three words can sum up all boss's feelings about this: DRUGS ARE DUMB; or maybe four words: DRUGS ARE REAL DUMB. Any kind of a hangover from drugs, even prescription ones, is a curse to the workplace. Bosses despise it, even if they're guilty of it themselves. Drugs reduce and limit employee function and burden the boss. The boss doesn't have the time and money to rehabilitate anyone or schedule around their "down times." Drugs will be the eventual undoing of your job—guaranteed—if you keep using them. Me and most of my associates are avoiding hiring even tobacco smokers anymore. We may like the person, but we don't like the habit, nor do we want the burden of safety and health hazards in our operations. You wouldn't either. Drugs cut production time terribly, affect other workers, and cause accidents and security problems. And like most bosses I'm extra careful not to reveal confidential matters to those who through the drug called alcohol have the loose lips that sink ships.

Constant use of even legal drugs can be a liability in some work environments. Antacids, painkillers, and other over-the-counter remedies as well as prescription medications may occasionally be necessary, but between me and you, I'd practice privacy with them. I wouldn't line them all up on the desktop.

Those Perks and Benefits

Companies made a desperate effort a few years back to attract workers and outdo their competitors by upping and upping and upping their benefits. To the point that what benefits a company offered got to be more the question than what the job was and what it might mean to the whole future of one's life. Being taken care of became more the focus than taking care of business.

Now after assuming the responsibility for not only employee wealth but health, welfare, education, teeth, hearing aid batteries, pensions, pregnancies, home buyouts, moves, and all sorts of golden parachutes and other security measures, companies are getting the backlash of it all. Insurance rates, government regulatory paperwork and reports, etc., have turned these employee aids into an expensive, cumbersome negative; a legal, accounting and financial hassle for bosses.

The other day a young woman came to me looking for work and the first words out of her mouth were: "I need a good health plan for my family. Can I go to work for you to get one? I knew she was an excellent worker, but she was out. Benefits were established to assist employees, not run their whole lives for them. Your job is not intended to manage your whole life, but to give you the resources to do it yourself, in exchange for your time.

Times are changing... CUT THE FAT is the byword of business everywhere. Even the largest and best-established companies can no longer afford to pay big bucks for mere seniority or bureaucrats. No production, no job or benefits. One major company just retired 300 senior vice presidents and didn't replace them. The current rule in business is: If you want benefits, you better be worth it!

Should you expect the boss to train you?

The kid showed up on the construction site holding an ad for a backhoe job. "Are you an operator?" the boss asked. "No, but I want to be, you can train me and I'll do a good job." "Tell you what," the grizzled foreman said, "you go home or to school or somewhere and learn to dig with one of these things and I'll hire you." The kid was incensed when he heard this, and said "It's your job to train me." The wise old foreman then spoke a great truth: "I pay people to do the work, not to learn how—you learn on your own time."

For the most part, at home is the place where we learn how to do it, and the workplace is where we do it and get paid for it. We can't expect the boss to pay us to learn, unless we're already working there and they get a new machine or position that requires special training.

If you aren't willing to invest in yourself, you'll be the loser in the end. Whether you're cleaning floors, building cars, or managing money, you need to be better than others. You can only do that by continuing to learn, it's the only real guarantee of future employment.

The difference between what you get and what you cost

I remember how shocked I was in high school when I discovered that a new Chevy advertised for $2500 cost $3800 when you drove it out of the dealer's lot. False advertising? Nope, it's base price was $2500. It was all the extras—power steering, air conditioning, radio, pin striping, undercoat, side mirrors, etc.—that accounted for the extra $1300. Likewise, lots of us see our wage or salary (say it's $8.00 an hour) as what we are costing our boss. The truth is, he or she is also paying a lot more.

What you cost the boss

An hourly wage of $8.00 an hour is actually $10.47+, by the time you add in the cost of benefits and overhead, such as Social Security tax, Medicare, state and federal unemployment tax, Worker's Compensation, liability insurance, 401K and retirement plans, cafeteria plans, administration of benefits, training, payroll processing and record keeping, etc.

I had a crew, once, that went out on a window cleaning job at $5.00 an hour each. It was an $85 job and it took them 3 hours. Back at the shop the head guy confronted me and said, "This isn't fair, Mr. Aslett, we worked on that job three hours, and there were three of us, so that means 9 x $5.00. That's $45 and you got $85, so you made $40.00, and you didn't even do the work." It did appear that way to him, since was unaware of all the boss's costs. So I set a notepad down on the table in front of him and asked him:

"Where did the job come from, did it just jump into your hands? "
"No, I advertised for it."

Share of our advertising cost allotted to this job	**1.40**
"Who lined it up?"	
Cost of an office person for 1/4 hour plus the phone	**2.40**
"Who bid it?"	
Cost of one hour of my time to drive out and bid it	**12.00**
"How did you do the job?"	
Cost of truck, gas, insurance for 20 miles	**8.00**
Plus a share of the cost of ladders, squeegees, cleaning solution, etc., needed to do the job	**1.12**
Wages (counting travel time, a total of 4 hours)	**60.00**
30% payroll tax	**18.00**
TOTAL EXPENSES	**$102.92**
Income	85.00
	-$17.92

I let him add up the total himself, and the result was clear to both of us: *"You guys cost me money—I lost $17.92 on this job—you were too slow!"*

This is the biggest surprise to workers who go out and start their own business, this thing called hidden costs. They aren't hidden long, I can assure you. They will soon appear, with the aid of government agencies, to squeeze every dime out of your profits. You usually have to add 30 or 40% to the cost of your wages for the costs of carrying you in the company, for everything from heat to health care. So take whatever you get paid and add a third more—that's what you really cost the boss!

Many company owners could at this very minute make more money by selling their business and living off the interest. I could right now, too. Then why do we stay with it and keep running it? We enjoy it and feel responsible for the people who work for us.

Vacations and holidays

Employees love days off, holidays, and vacation!

Bosses don't.

Before you judge bosses to be heartless, insensitive, or "workaholics," let me enlighten you on a few things that will help both you and the boss enjoy your days off more.

First, you are going to hear, from all the bosses in your life, some whining about no days off of their own. "I haven't taken a vacation in thirty years," or "I worked all day Thanksgiving." Millions of bosses and owners do this, and it's our own doing. We can take all the days off and vacations we want, but we don't. Why? Because most bosses are so interested and motivated by their work, they don't want time off. They love working extra, they choose it that way.

But those of you who aren't getting the bonuses, promises of future rewards, and satisfaction of ownership that the boss is, may not share the boss's enthusiasm to work every minute possible. And you may feel a little guilty sometimes about taking off when the boss has to stay and work. Those days off and vacations are well earned and you should take them and feel darn good about it, too. There are just a few little things that bother bosses about these official times away from work. Let me clue you in on what they are, so you can feel even better about heading out the door.

We bosses don't resent your joyful leaving, nor the fun you have baking on the beach, racing down the slopes, rooting at the ballgame, or just lounging in bed on your days off. It's the *spillover* that dampens bosses'

enthusiasm. A few years ago, for instance, both Christmas and New Year's Day fell on Thursday. For each of those two days and for every one of the eight other legal holidays I give all my salaried people, I pay about $43,000 a day. In this case not only the actual days off, but the day before each, Christmas and New Year's Eve, were "time off the job." People came in but no one worked—they partied, played, arranged last-minute gifts, ate and drank, and called friends and relatives to extend the greetings of the season. Same with the days right after each of the holidays, the interruptions were incredible and nothing got done either of those days either. I personally paid out at least $100,000 in those two weeks over and beyond the holidays themselves, for no work done.

Then too, in the strapped start-up years of my company, I can remember employees in a lot better financial shape than the boss lined up with long faces waiting for the Christmas bonus they were banking on, or for the use of a company vehicle or condo for their holiday trips. So Bah! Humbug! can be easy for a boss to say at Christmas.

No wonder larger companies simply close down all operations from Christmas Eve day through New Year's Day. It saves them money by not having to pay for an inefficient operation during this 10 day holiday season.

I have salaried people who not only take their vacation, which I pay fully for, but snatch one or two days before and after to recover, return rentals, etc. It's that arranging of things and talking to twelve others about it for a week before and reporting on it the whole week after that ticks off bosses, not the days you are gone.

Fairness regarding those fine days off will make you feel better and the boss less frowny!

Keep your personal finances private

Your personal finances are indeed personal and not the worry or business of your boss or the workplace. Don't bring your financial affairs, good or bad, to the job.

Even in the early days of my business, employees who managed their money poorly, who couldn't make it from paycheck to paycheck, would often come whimpering to me for an "advance." I was struggling worse than they were, but I'd do it if I could. An advance is basically a loan, and most of them got so used to it they needed that cash infusion every month. This was a real pain for the payroll department, and few of the people involved ever thanked me for it. They just figured that getting money ahead, before they'd earned it, was a privilege they deserved. The bigger my company grew, the more advances I gave, trying to help my people with their financial problems. It never really did. One day on the year-end balance sheet I noticed we had $23,000 in bad debts under "Advances," employees who never paid it back, just took it and took off. We eventually tightened our advance policy to only those who had special problems. Guess how many that turned out to be—yup, 100%. One hundred percent of the people asking for advances claimed they qualified under special need. That was the last straw. The new policy was: No advances under any circumstance, and we held to it. And guess what? Things improved for both the company and for them. We took this crutch away, and because they were forced to, they became better handlers of their own money (which was their responsibility all along, not the boss's).

Don't try to use your employer to bail out your personal finances. It will hurt both him and you. Even *asking* for advances irritates both the boss and the accounting department.

Another worthwhile rule I probably don't have to tell you is: Keep your pay, raises, bonuses, etc., to yourself. Paying fairly is a struggle for a boss, no two people are worth exactly the same, even doing the same job. Yet most employers pay in classes and categories. Lots of times, to even things up for someone who really broke their butt, I'll give them an extra $100 or $500. Then, unfortunately, they just have to announce it on the public address system, rub it in to everyone in hearing distance. Now all the undeserving (who by the way are always the first to believe they are the deserving) scream and moan. And the boss loses ground for trying to help someone gain ground.

Likewise many good people complain their way out of a job, like one secretary in our company who did payroll during the absence of a payroll clerk and found out several people she didn't think should, were making more than her. What others make will only be a poison to you, don't ever worry about it.

Your pay, your bank account, your bills, your investments are your personal and private affairs. Keeping them that way on the job will be an advantage. Revealing your financial problems to the boss or co-workers only makes you look incompetent, and going on about your successes and financial windfalls only makes you sound like a braggart, or like you don't need the job anymore.

Your way or the highway

We all have our own personal rule book and code of conduct, our own set of standards and ways of doing things, our likes and dislikes and will do's and won't do's. Fortunately in our private lives and all our personal dealings, we can usually operate according to our scruples. That's fine and good and admirable and entirely within our rights as Americans, as long as we don't violate anyone else's privacy or territory.

When we go to work for someone else, however, we always have to make some adjustments in this well learned and liked system of ours. So don't get excited, belligerent, or too quick on the trigger when you run into a conflict between your rules and the company's or the boss's. Something has to give if they don't agree. Maybe you like to sleep in till noon and then work hard till midnight. But the job says you have to be there at 5:30 a.m. and get off at 2:30. The terms and conditions of any job are seldom exactly suited to any of us. When something runs against your grain or your personal rule book, sit down and think it over before you decide to make a big deal about it. Consider the alternatives—what you're giving up vs. what you're gaining and who is in the controlling position at the moment. And then conform to the boss's rules and live by them, or look for somewhere else closer to your rules.

Whatever you do, don't expect big companies and customers and the sun and moon to adjust themselves to you—it won't happen.

What if the boss makes a mistake?

Sometimes it seems that the boss's way isn't your way or the right way, either. Before you get yourself all worked up, make sure you're seeing things clearly: It could be that the boss's way is actually the right one and yours is wrong.

Bosses do make mistakes—some of them in fact may make many more than you do. But inaccuracy doesn't dilute authority. The boss is still the boss, and her way of doing things should be followed, not questioned. If you do see an error (and are sure of it), politely and quietly bring it to the boss's attention. Most bosses will love you for it. And now *keep still* about it. Don't go blabbing all over how you saved or outsmarted the boss!

On being one of the team

The school's big choir production was widely advertised and tirelessly practiced, and then presented in the finest hall in the county. The sounds were perfect, but the overall effect was poor, all because one striking redhead in the soprano section had to be an individualist in this team effort. A choir needs to work and move as one, but she flashed smiles and struck poses, moved as provocatively as possible, tilted her head, bounced and shifted her body, waved to friends, and all in all was so distracting it just ruined the whole effect.

We all love individualism, being personable, unique, fresh, and original. But most of the time in a work force, as in the ranks of a precision Army march or a football team on the field of play, this isn't the time or place for total freedom of feeling or conduct.

Don't be afraid of tough rules

A nationally known chain store moved to our town, and the first thing I heard from all the locals who applied for work was what stringent, hard-nosed policies the store had. In short, no frills and no exceptions. You either did the job the way they wanted it done or you were out of there, gone, fired. After long years of experience the store had learned that leniency only invited the employees to lean on them, and so they were forced to set and enforce rules—tough ones.

As I listened to all the criticism and complaints from all the deadbeats who got washed out, I noticed something I wouldn't have believed if I hadn't seen it with my own

Some attitudes to abandon

- This company is sure lucky to have me...
- The boss or company owes me...
- I did ______ and so I'm entitled to...
- This operation better fit me...
- I don't like the way they do things around here...

And a Big BIG **BIG** final one:

- *The boss is to blame for all my problems*...

Few of us can or will own up to our problems. We just don't like fault or blame and so we need to find a victim, a scapegoat, *someone* who's caused us to be poor, miserable, indecisive. Someone who causes the problems with our love life and our health, someone who is shattering our nerves and stressing us, blocking our pro-gress and promotion, someone who is re-sponsible for the rotten deals we get in life.

Believe it or not, many people do blame all this on work or the boss. Who else do they have? Other blamables like the government, teachers, parents, the police, the landlord, their spouse, God, etc., won't take the blame, or have already been overused. But the boss is perfect. So they start believing and living that way. Some people do this their whole lives long, come home and complain and moan and whimper to themselves, their family and friends about how their job and their boss is totally wrecking their lives, holding them up and keeping them back. The boss becomes their lifelong torturer.

Rarely is this true, and you'll waste a lifetime trying to convince yourself and others. Don't get caught in this trap!

eyes. Some of the slowest, dullest, laziest people around, the ones with the worst work attitudes (the ones we'd all pegged as losers around the community), stayed and held their jobs and were like transformed beings. They became quick, polite, appreciative, and even cheerful and happy! I never realized some of them even had a pulse. And now here they were, working for this tough chain store, as number ones—I mean *good* workers. Some that I was sure were lost causes even became bosses and supervisors!

It was all the result of tough rules and policies—in the military they keep you safe and alive, in church they keep you kind and active, and at work they keep the company solvent. Don't fight tough rules, they work in your favor. Just get tougher.

On remembering which side of the counter you're on

We are there at work to serve customers, not be one. Way too often we cross the line, trying on the clothes we should be selling, eating the food we should be serving, driving the car we should be fixing. Customers and clients hate it when we break ranks. No one wants to be playing a round of golf and be held up on the eighth hole by a group of caddies goofing around on the course.

Let's imagine, for another example, that you and your friend go to dinner at the city's finest restaurant. The setting is elegant, the food superb, and then suddenly out of the kitchen come three chefs and a short-order cook on their break. They're all in grease-stained whites as they clamour around the table right next to you and have an enthusiastic feast and rousing conversation. Isn't this okay? After all, they're just as good as you, they've earned their break, and they're hungry. But they're out of place, and they offend the guests.

Once you're in the harness or have on the uniform to work, that separates you from the public. Until it's off, you're not free to talk and act just like them.

Loyalty—or not biting the hand that feeds you

The first time I ever saw the word loyalty it was squeezed in between "trustworthy" and "brave" in the Scout pledge. Around the campfire, loyalty was explained to me as the most binding virtue of a relationship. You don't need to memorize all the laws of scouting to work for someone, but knowing and practicing just that one—loyalty—will go a long way toward forging a good strong relationship between you and your boss. To be loyal you don't have to have a company sticker on both bumpers, wear a company sweatshirt while you're jogging, sing the company song in the shower, sport your company watch, or stand in the front row cheering your boss in the parade (even though it doesn't hurt to do so). True loyalty is a simple, subtle, but always active endorsement of your boss and his goals.

If you want some examples of what loyalty ***ISN'T***:

- You walk into the lobby of a major ABC affiliate, and the receptionist is watching CBS.
- You count the cars in a parking lot for GM employees, and 60% are foreign makes.
- You're a Kodak PR manager, but you don't mind using Fuji film.
- You work in a well-known clothing store, but buy your clothes in a competitor's store, and let it be known that you do.
- You work in a diet and health center, but you smoke and are carrying quite a few extra pounds.
- You've got a great summer job and lots of benefits at Sizzler, but refuse to eat there, and in fact make a point of taking all your friends to Arby's.

Your reaction to these examples may be: 1. The boss doesn't own me; 2. I put in my time, and what I do on my own personal time is my own business; 3. I have total rights and freedom off the job. All of these statements are right—you can eat where you want, drive what you want, live as you wish, watch what you want—as long as you do your job, legally that's all you owe.

By the same logic, however, your boss could say, "All I owe you is a paycheck for exactly the hours you work." Likewise the boss doesn't owe you perks—bonuses, extra time off, raises, promotions, health plans, etc. All of these are options he or she pays extra for out of what would be company profits.

Beyond that, to get down to real basics, loyalty is not biting the hand that feeds you, putting yourself 100% behind a person or a company as long as you're taking their money. Loyalty will go a long way toward pleasing your boss and preserving your job. It's doing all you can on and off the job to enhance the operation. It's knowing, and being proud of, who you work for and what they do.

This means you don't want to be like the young woman I hired once. After she worked for me for several months, she was nominated for Miss Harvest Queen. The whole company was proud of her—she had a big interview on the radio and we all listened. The host asked her name and the usual family questions and then: "Who do you work for?"

"Don Aslett."

"What does he do?"

Silence. And then finally: "I don't know."

The fact that loyalty to our country, good causes of all kinds, religion, and the family unit is at an all-time low doesn't excuse lack of loyalty in the workplace. It's just another reason to practice some loyalty to your job and your boss—it just might spill back over into some of those other areas.

Bad-mouthing the boss

You've heard the old advice, "Don't bite the hand that feeds you," well let's go one better: Don't poop in it either!

As a young woman recounted to me once: "I was employed for quite a while in a huge company—there were 4,000 people in the main office where I worked. I was just a youngster then, and it really amazed me that half of the employees spent at least 40% of their time griping about the company: repeating, and elaborating on common criticisms of the company, making snide remarks and jokes about the company, etc. etc. All I could ever think was: "If you think this place is so awful, why are you working here? You either have no ambition, or you don't care who or what you're associated with."

Don't we all hear people every day griping and moaning and criticizing the company that's feeding them? Pure hypocrisy. When they're asked, "If you hate this place so much, why do you work here?" we get a real gutless answer, "Well, I need the money." Or "They've got good benefits."

Now I ask you, what kind of person would want to destroy the very source of her sustenance? Who would be low enough to take money from someone they're cheating? (Oral nonsupport is cheating because it cuts production.) If you were drafted into the army, no choice about it, you might have the right to make a few bitches, but even so, in a lot of armies they shoot you for speaking against the cause or the captain!

Bad-mouthing your boss or the company is shooting yourself in the foot, for you can count on it getting back to the boss. Or at break, some quiet person in the group where you are singing your sad head off will be your next boss. You've planted the seeds of trouble that may take years to sprout. And even if *you* are made boss after being "Bitcher of the Year," you'll never regain the respect of your comrades.

If you're unhappy, and a real man or woman, you'll activate your feet, not your jaw. Don't shoot down the system that's serving up your paycheck.

Always level with your boss

"If I tell the boss during this initial interview that I'll be leaving at the end of the summer, he won't hire me, so I just won't say anything, and pretend I'm taking the job for the long haul. Then I'll leave in September, and at least I'll have a good job for the summer."

This sort of thing is the one of the worst things you can do to an employer. He or she will eventually know the truth, and what damage they won't do you in the future (when they share this fact with future prospective employers), you'll do to yourself... because you know you're a liar.

I'm not saying you have to bare your soul to the boss or the company. But do inform them of things that are going to pop up unexplained someday, or which might have a

bearing on your job (or your ability to do it). Such as:

- •A prison record
- •A bad driving record
- •A chronic illness
- •A dangerous hobby
- •A crazy ex
- •An extra business on the side
- •The fact that you carry a firearm
- •Special religious days you will have to observe
- •Color blindness
- •Acute paranoia or other serious mental conditions
- •The fact that you have a "small bladder" (humph!)

Never underestimate what your boss knows

Most of them have worn out the trail you're now traveling for the first time, have memorized signs and scenery you haven't seen yet.

Sometimes you'll hear "The boss is the last to know," or "The boss doesn't know what's going on," and that might be true, but notice no one says "The boss will never know."

Someone, sometime, tells the boss everything.

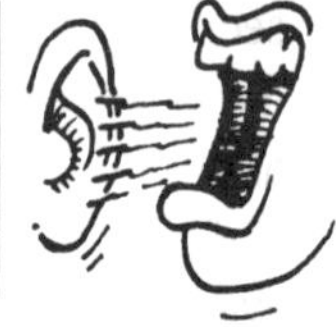

In fact it's amazing, we bosses never have to ask. People are just dying to tell the power source what all the subjects are up to. Bosses aren't "big brothers," they don't ask or snoop. All kinds of information about their business and their personnel just flows to them free of charge.

I'll be in a restaurant in Texas, for example, and learn the very afternoon it happens that two of my managers in Washington have gone off on a camping trip with company vehicles, or that my regional supervisor has just charged his personal new VCR on the company account, or that George wasn't sick, he went to the UCLA game. Next to God (and your parents when you're little) the boss knows, or finds out, more than anyone. And finding out later is always worse than an immediate tip-off.

Bosses always find out who rips them off, who says bad things about them, who slacks when they're out of sight.

That goes for your good works, too

For the same reason, you don't need to sit around thinking: *The boss doesn't notice me, my brilliant work....*

When I first began touring to publicize my books, there were times when I was out of the office two thirds of the time, traveling all over the U.S., Canada, and abroad. Our corporate secretary Debbie did some jobs for me, but didn't work directly for me. One Friday afternoon she popped her head into my office and said, "Mr. Aslett, I'm all caught up and even a little ahead of myself, is there something I can do for you, even errands or anything? I said "Debbie, you've worked like crazy all week, it's a slow day, it's 3:00 p.m., you've got a big weekend planned. You came in early all last week and worked late on Monday and Thursday, so why don't you take the rest of the day off? I'll get your calls."

She didn't move, and tears began to roll down her cheeks. "How did you know I did that extra?" I stood up then and rattled off all her short lunches, early arrivals, and late work over the last month, plus several compliments I'd heard on her work. She was overwhelmed.

This impressed Debbie, but it wouldn't impress other bosses much. Most of them could do the same thing. Good bosses develop a telepathy for what's going on, at the office, at home, or away. What they don't see, feel, absorb, or make it a point to find out, someone tells them. It's almost spooky. I'm no mental giant when it comes to math, but I've always been able to astound our accountants, secretaries, and payables and receivables people. With a total of $50,000 out on the books, they could just read me an amount due, and I could give them the name and age of the account. Same with the money we owed, even if it was $3.14 I knew who to and what for. They thought it was amazing, because they worked with these figures every day, and I was just in and out a couple of times a week. It's not a Houdini trick, almost any boss can do it. There is a little magic in it though—whatever you answer for, becomes a part of you. And that includes those who work for you.

Extracurricular company activities

Once aboard most jobs, you'll be approached for all kinds of activities which are not required of you nor part of the job, but could weigh heavily in the view of you as an employee. (Especially if you happen to be a 6' 8" ex-college all-star and your company is into softball, football, volleyball, etc.) Same with clubs and organizations and professional associations. While I was a teacher in high school, it was the NEA (National Education Association) that everyone was supposed to join. It wasn't mandatory, but it looked good on your record. I was the only teacher in the district who didn't join, because I'm not much of one for social stuff. My boss didn't like it,

but after I explained it he honored my decision and my reason.

Things like this are entirely up to you. Just be wise when you're considering them and don't always think of yourself first. You might hate to bowl, but welding relationships might be worth spending a Wednesday night out with the company.

If you do make or take a stand unpopular in the eyes of others, be sure to give a good reason and explain your side of it. This will generally defuse the worst wrath.

What about the company picnic?

Yes, I'd go, and not act too stupid. And yes, if I could best the boss in anything, from a race to wrestling, I wouldn't hold back, I'd do it as hard as I could. In the long run they'll love you for it. It might not seem like a good political move, but it is....

Socializing on the job

How friendly should you be with the public and your fellow workers while at work? If you don't say a word and just keep your nose to the grindstone, you'll appear to be giving everyone the cold shoulder. If you wave, gab, and visit with everyone you encounter, on the other hand, you'll never get any work done and the boss will think of you as a glad hander. This is a tricky area, because we all know that a simple "Good Morning" or "How are you?" can trigger a full-fledged health report and family history from some people.

Too much friendliness on the job can put off the public, too. The line between service and socializing is a fine one. Most bosses don't want a whole company full of employees who think they were hired for PR, and yet they want them to be warm and friendly. We need to be guided by instinct here, because situations are so different and the ground rules are so vague. But you can find a middle ground.

When I was nineteen, for example, I carried the U.S. and intercomplex mail for a Union Pacific resort. I had a long route and if I was delayed anywhere I'd fall behind schedule and have an angry boss. Yet the boss gave me the instruction to "be warm and friendly to the guests and clients." I had 48 stops to make at offices and shops, plus probably a thousand individuals in between. The rule of thumb I made for myself was: smile broadly and make a briefly friendly remark ("Good morning!" "Cold, huh?" or "Thank you") while always *keeping moving.* If you stopped for a second they'd glue you down. With motion came freedom. I've practiced this technique right up to today. I don't have a chair in my office for anyone to sit in—if I want them to stay and visit and socialize I go get a chair.

Different jobs do call for different degrees of employee friendliness. Find out where your boss stands when it comes to this. I've always found "friendly " far better than "familiar" when it comes to personal interactions in the workplace.

Keep it brief and stay in motion!

Don't ignore the dress code

"What I look like is my own business" works fine when we're about our own affairs, but not when we're under contract to work for and around someone else. Whether we like it or not, they now have the right to approve what we wear and how we look. If you can't live with that, it's not going to be easy to earn a living. The job site is not the place to be different, to make a statement, to show off your money or your nerve or your muscle, or reveal your bumps and bulges, positive or negative.

Your job isn't the place to show up with two days' macho growth of beard, even if Bruce Willis and Tom Cruise are getting away with it. For the most part, trends offend! Bosses are right in there with everyone else who hates show-offs and exhibitionism, and they hate it because all of this is a distraction not only for the colleagues and the customers, but for the person sporting it.

Too much, too little, too dirty, ill fitting, or bad color choice are all a liability on the job. It might be against your religion to take baths, cut hair, or wear shoes. If so, then I'd suggest you find a job at a monastery or mine or somewhere where cleanliness and grooming aren't so important. Bosses love neatness, clean cut, conservative, etc. Bad or "way out" appearance of any kind drives customers and business away from the workplace. When that happens, they don't need you to work there. So look good and dress well. If the company requires uniforms, don't even sniff, just select one that fits well and make yourself look sharp in it.

"Well no one sees me," you say, "so why does it matter what I look like?" Well the boss and other workers see you, and you see yourself. Tough judges, because all three have a heavy hand in whether you're promoted or not.

The other extreme, the "too pretty to work problem"

After waiting in a long and irritated line at a pizza maker's convention in Las Vegas, I got to the counter and beheld a beautiful young woman pouring fruit juice samples. I could see the problem immediately—this lovely lady, a local model, was hired by the pizza association to pour the juice. But her gorgeous (or grotesque) fingernails were so long and awkward she couldn't separate the paper cups in the stack, and so had to fumble, pick, and pry for each one. She was worthless for that job, overgroomed, you might say.

We all occasionally show up in clothes, or shoes, or hairdos that limit our ability to work. It's nice to look nice, but when it detracts from your ability to do your job, you shouldn't have to be told. Examples:

1. Clothes you wouldn't dare soil, or that are too tight or too short to move in.
2. Shoes too flimsy, high heeled, open toed, etc., for the job at hand.
3. Jewelry that could get caught in the machinery.
4. Too much cleavage or hairy chest, etc. showing.
5. A hairstyle that's sure to mean hair in the food.

Company rules

Here, the golden rule applies, again, maybe a little different version than the one you've heard: "He with the gold rules." In every business you'll find some rules you don't like, and maybe some you hate. If you can't live with the rules of a job, then don't take it, or keep it. Rules are what hold an organization together. Keeping the rules (or only keeping the ones you happen to like) is not an option. When you're at work, you can't and don't make the rules, and for sure all rules won't fit you 100%. That's life in the workplace. Quietly and calmly withdraw if you have to, but never fight the rules. It hurts the boss and the business.

While I was teaching school, teachers had the privilege of going to the front of the lunch line. I dislike "line jumping," so I refused to go to the front of the line and stood in line with the students (which they loved). This put some heat on the rest of the teachers: "Hey, how come you can cut in and we can't?" Things got a little tense and the principal (my boss) finally came to me and told me I *would* go to the front of the line like all my colleagues. So I could respect his policy without breaking my own personal rules, I carried my lunch to school after that in a paper sack... no big deal.

Is what I do on my own time any of the boss's business?

Maybe. If on your day off, for example, you rescue a school bus full of children and are recognized nationally as a heroine, what you did on your own time sure reflects on your boss and your job, in this case in a positive way:

> **WOMAN DIVES IN RIVER, SAVES 73**
> Ms. Day, a resident of Updale, dish drainer designer for the nearby Rubbermaid factory, was...

Something like this is a morale builder and gives your boss and your co-workers a real boost. If, on the other hand, you were the drunk driver who swerved over the median strip and ran the school bus into the river, and the media mentions where you happen to work, you could actually injure your boss and the company.

Most bosses are concerned about what goes on in your personal life, as it will always be reflected in, and carry over to, your job life. If you abuse your family, use drugs all night, or drink all weekend, it's going to affect

not only your ability to work, but the image of the company you project on Monday morning. If your job puts you in a position to teach and guide young people, or to represent the company to ultra-conservative customers, your boss will not be anxious to learn that you are the hottest lover in this corner of the state.

Little things can have a bad effect here, too, such as bumper stickers that say "Take This Job and Shove It" or "Honk If You're Horny" even "Thank God It's Friday" or "I'm in No Hurry, I'm on My Way to Work."

Even in sports now, note how important off-field or off-court conduct and activities have become. Even star players who win games but are jerks, druggies, con men, or lawbreakers off the field lose a lot of their edge with the public as well as their employers.

The Fine Line Between Fun and Fooling Around

(Horseplay... can give us a kick in the head)

Nobody wants to see an employee with a sour face or a grumpy attitude. When you're alive, enthusiastic, vibrant, humorous, and even capable of a joke or two... more power to you. Personality helps keep the wheels of business turning. A little good-natured interplay with each other when we're working, and even with the customers or clients (careful here) is great. However—and this is crucial—it has to be in good taste. You were hired for your horsepower and horse sense, not for horseplay. So think before pulling stunts that might backfire or injure someone.

Here are a few of the biggies to be aware of:

Notes

If you ever write one that contains any crudeness or anger, criticism or profanity, I promise you it will be preserved and pulled forth forever to haunt you. Keep any written correspondence with clients or *anyone* cordial, positive, nonjudgmental, and free of threats of any kind, and you'll keep your job and your self-respect.

Tricks and Gags

We've all booby trapped something sometime. set up a surprise display, or a hot-pepper sauce, etc., to get a reaction out of the rest of the crew or our clients. Keep any little tricks positive and loving and strictly for a laugh. Always ask yourself first: Is this safe, physically and emotionally, for others and for me?

Scuffles

I've seen full-grown men suddenly acting like two competing bulls in spring—start scuffling (usually good-naturedly), slapping and cuffing and wrestling with each other. If the urge for a little roughhousing is overwhelming, go to the weight room or outside or to a gym somewhere. Slips and falls while fooling around can cost you a lot of pain and heartbreak and your boss a lot of liability.

Equipment and Machinery

Use it only as intended. Races with forklifts or mail carts or serving carts, sword fights with brooms or mops (I'm giving you all kinds of ideas, right?), dueling with spray bottles filled with cleaning chemicals, spinning off chairs, playing flying saucer with garbage can lids or the cookware, is pretty exhilarating and does break up the day a little, but it will also break up the building, desks, fixtures, etc.

Knowing the difference between passion and compassion

Most of us show our best side at work. We dress better, look better, smell better, and act nicer. Men and women see each other in the best possible light at work, so the workplace is ripe for romance, legal and illegal. And because the boss owns and runs the place, he or she carries a lot of responsibility for any carrying on. Anyone who decides to be a big macho man or the hottest little number at work is just a pain for the boss. No boss really likes someone using his or her facilities for hanky-panky, or even honest romance.

I know you feel your love life is none of the boss's business, but it is when it's at or around his place. It's strange, but any blame or repercussions over a workplace fling have a way of focussing more on where it happened than on who or why. An office romance is also a big distraction for all the other workers who may have dull lives. The gossiping, predicting, and analyzing others indulge in is usually more intense than the couple involved. A giant waste of time and emotion! Then too, the boss knows that after the affair is over, one or both of the former partners may quit, relations between their respective departments will now be strained and more.

The bottom line is... a kiss costs more at work, on the job, than in your private time and place. Watch it... avoid it!

One step up now

As for making a play for the boss, it ranks right in there with petting a rattlesnake—someone is bound to be bitten. (Even and especially if the boss initiates it.)

No amount of money, position, ownership, authority, age, or brilliance exempts a person from weakness. In fact, bosses are often even more lonely and motivated than most in this department. When it comes to romance, the boss's imagination can always go farther than their limitations, just like the lowliest office worker.

An otherwise strong-willed boss can invite you into their confidence and life, and before long, their bed. **Most** of the time, this will produce problems you won't be able to sleep off. It may start with a wink and end up a lot more than you can handle.

If the boss is legal game, and you want him or her to notice you, work may appear to be as good a place as any to catch a mate, looking at it from a strictly personal standpoint. But in most romances we do lose our head a little, and leadership and authority can get pretty confusing when people start dealing from the heart instead of the head. If you get the boss you might live happily ever after, but you run about a 95% chance of not succeeding, and in the process all the other employees will come to hate you. The boss's family will hate you, too, and the boss, once he or she has been involved with you, can never be objective again, no matter what dealings they have with you. Should you be promoted or not, get a raise or not, better assignment or not, all will always be questionable because that's what happens when questionable conduct has occurred.

Let me remind you again that at work we all see each other at our best—behavior, dress, manners, etc. and so the "other person" always appears better than what we have at home or are dating. I remember one of my employees, for instance, a sharp lady, brilliant, and a breath of fresh air just to be around. She was flawless, and she could get a deep sigh out of me just by walking by. When I finally had a good business reason to call her at home, I could hear two kids crying in the background. I knew she had kids but hearing them cry kind of shattered and shocked me. I had to chuckle because no way would I have believed she could have crying kids like the rest of us.

All that glitters in the workplace isn't gold. So don't be bold. Be careful.

Too often, we fall in love with the image and position and the power and not the person.

Your family and friends

You love them, and they may be smart and good looking, as well as honest, upstanding, brave, clean, and reverent. But bringing them on or around the job is not a good idea. It's too close to bringing your personal problems to work. 95% of the people you work for, for example, even those who love children and have six kids themselves, will be offended if you bring one of your own children on the job with you. Or even have a family member sit there and read quietly while you work. Or worse yet, have them help you. When someone is not officially hired the liability risks for safety and security are so great that your boss or management is bound to be uptight and irritated. This only leads to negative feelings about you. Bringing buddies along to help, even if they aren't getting paid, is out of line, no matter how right it may seem to you. In a few rare cases (I've known of a few), it can serve a constructive purpose when a family member comes to work with you. But the rule in professional cleaning, for example, is that if they don't work in the building as a regular scheduled crew member, they shouldn't be there.

This may seem a little harsh, but trust me, it isn't. It only makes good sense for all of us. I can give you some good reasons why from my own company's experience.

One little six-year-old, for instance, got tangled in some stage ropes while his father was cleaning, and hung himself. Other children have started fires or pushed the fire button while playing and panicked half the town. Things like having water fights or playing hide and seek in the lobby may seem innocent, but can cause damage and injury, too. Older children and teens will often use and misuse the phones or computers. And more "friends" than you would imagine will come in to the building with you and steal things. Or slip and fall on something, get into fights, or get lost.

Even if they don't pose any threat to themselves or their surroundings, we can be sure that the presence of our loved ones will do nothing for our concentration on the job at hand. In most jobs today it's our brainpower we're selling, and we can't give the company much of that when 80% of our brain cells are occupied with where the baby is wandering now or what sister Sue is saying.

I'm not talking about when long lost friends or your folks or grandfolks come through town and you ask them to come by the workplace for a few minutes to meet the boss and see where you work. These are "guests" and bosses like guests. But they don't like a spouse or close friend showing up early to pick you up and then tapping their fingers or pacing around in the lobby or outside your cubicle, as you hustle to get the mail out, or that final job done. Or parking right outside the back door or otherwise in the way, revving their motor and honking, as if you were sinning to work your shift out. Guests are welcome, but regular hangers-on or hangers-out will hang you!

Lots of bosses, likewise, are besieged by mothers and fathers who can't let their kids be on their new job—they have to call several times a week to check things out and evaluate them. If you have overprotective parents, ask them to cool it! Concern is okay, direct contact with your employer over YOUR job isn't, except maybe in an emergency.

While we're on this subject, bear in mind that you usually don't have the right to extend company privileges such as permits, passes, rides, and dorm rooms, to personal friends. Asking a friend to ride along with you en route to or delivering something somewhere in a company vehicle is taboo, even if you have six empty seats. Too much freedom with company fringes is a quick way to court suspicion or suspension.

You can't hide these things, either. You take the kids along in a emergency once and

nothing bad happens. So you're tempted to do it again, and then again, and then regularly, and then... something always happens. Many an executive has come in some morning and found animal cracker crumbs on the seat of his leather chair, where your two-year-old left them. When that sooner or later something does happen, who will have to answer for it? You. Often when you're called in to answer for it you won't even have been aware that your buddy or girl or boy friend who came to work with you was tying up the phone, or using the copier. You'll be sick, and your job situation may be even sicker.

This is an easy one to cure. Just make a firm rule—no family or friends on the job with you. Then make it known and make no exceptions.

P.S. This goes for your furry family, too

For similar reasons, you also never want to bring your pets to work. You have enough to do there without worrying about which pile of papers they'll decide to play with, whether or not they'll remember their potty training, and where *did* your pet boa constrictor slither to?

Should you let your boss take the credit (or not)?

A great man once said, "You'll gain everything in life and great blessings for what you do, if you don't care who gets the credit." It works because 95% of the time, even when you give the credit for something you've done to others, everyone sooner or later knows or finds out *you* did it. Making your boss and colleagues look good isn't just kind and charitable. You'll feel good, they'll appreciate it, and yes, trust me, eventually everyone, even your boss's boss will find out it was you in the end and only respect and admire you more.

I learned this quickly doing national shows on TV. I had some great lines I'd worked up over the years to lead into cleaning questions. I found that if I passed them to the hosts during rehearsals, and told them when and how to use them, they were grateful. I made them look good... and notice I'm still in demand for their shows, while others who hogged all the lines and the glory are gone.

If you follow this philosophy, surprise, surprise, just when you need it most and least expect it, the boss will give you full credit and honor for something he or she thought up!

When you have something to say or ask

You don't have to be an employee anywhere long to find and store up some things to say about the place. Most of us can manage to accumulate more advice and opinion than we get—and that's a lot!

We all see things that irritate or even alarm us, and things we know could be improved. We may want to answer criticisms that've been directed at us, or need information, supplies, or equipment we don't have.

Who should we direct these things to, and how? Here are some guidelines I've learned along the way.

1. First, the Golden Rule: **Before you do anything, make sure you're right.**

Make sure your facts are up to date and accurate, and that what you have in mind is important and needed. Often when some little thing happens (we find a dead mouse in the coffee pot), we have the impulse to become the "town crier," or at least call Channel 5 Action News. *Think* before you report or talk—some things are best taken care of quietly and privately, or just left to blow over.

When "things aren't run right around here" (about the most common complaint of employees), you do want to let people know if you see something better that could be done, but be careful. Lots of the time things are run a lot better than you think and you just haven't had a chance to see how it all works yet. All you'll do is look dumb if you run to the boss with a long list of how he or she should be running things.

2. If you do decide to go forward, **always go to your own contact person first,** your supervisor or boss or the person who hired you. You always want to deal directly with them first. Skipping rank or going over people's heads is a deadly game that will get you in the end. The more people you approach or enlist before going to the right person, the more you will worsen and complicate things. And about the only value of rank anyway is to process communications properly. So go right to your boss, or at most, the next step up, not to fellow workers.

3. **Should you say it or write it?** You have your choice. Lately I'm swinging around to the written word. When it's right there on the page, it saves time hunting for someone or making appointments to see them. And once you write out a draft you can work on it a little if you need to, to make sure it says exactly what you want to say, no more and no less, and no unfortunate unanticipated slips of the tongue. On the other hand, anything written is lasting evidence, so if you accuse or profane or criticize someone it can stay around to haunt you forever. Some things should only be spoken.

4. **Keep your suggestions positive**. Bosses do appreciate constructive suggestions, but make sure yours are exactly that—that they're phrased or written up in a tactful and positive way. Don't just make a passing swipe because you're in a bad mood or think you've been treated badly. Provide solid information backed with evidence and your own commitment to help bring your proposal to pass. Have a positive attitude, and go to the boss with not just problems, but a possible solution or two. You'll be amazed how many things are worked out in minutes and even better than you dared hope!

Even if you have complaints, don't be a complainer. There are risks involved:
1. Your complaint might be aired to the wrong person
2. It might later prove to be invalid

5. **Tattling and tales**. A tough one! Should you report, or bring to your boss's attention, things they really should know about, though it might mean tattling on your buddies?

Divided loyalty is one of the biggest tests of any professional, and you're bound to be faced with some real conflicts. There's a torrid romance going on in your department, or your best friend is using the company computer illegally late at night. You don't want to be aware of or involved in any of this, but you are. What can you do? You can go on your merry way and things will get worse, and eventually someone may get fired, or divorced. Or is it better to tell? It's a tough, tough position to be in, and you'll be in it many times.

I would prepare myself for situations like this in advance by making it clear to my fellow workers where my loyalties lie. Those who are employing and paying me should have my loyalty, and if I can't give it to them then I shouldn't be working there. Once you've made that stand, others won't put you on the spot, because they'll already know that your first loyalty is to the company, your employer. Then when a problem comes up I'd inform my contact person in the company of what they need to know, for the good of the company and the preservation of *everyone's* job.

"If my best buddy is cheating on his time card or stealing stuff, should I rat on him? Shouldn't I be loyal to my friends, too?" The answer is easy: He or she is the rat, not you or the boss.

6. **What if the boss or the company doesn't take your advice?** One custodian who had fought a back door garbage problem for years, drew up a plan for the construction of the perfect retainer pad to eliminate the problem. Her supervisor loved it, but when they submitted it to headquarters they said "We don't take advice from custodians." So the garbage kept blowing around and the dogs kept rummaging in it. Undaunted, the custodian kept up her campaign for three years. Finally they did build it. It cost next to nothing and cured all the problems... and headquarters took all the credit for this brilliant idea.

If you do give the boss or company good advice and it's ignored, don't slash your wrists over it. The same thing that happens to smart custodians happens tens of thousands of times a year to CEO's, professors, mayors, and major league ball players. They didn't call it "red tape" for no reason. The red is for the blood let by contributing comrades who were ignored or had the credit robbed from them. It's happened to me right in the company I own, and it's happened to your boss too. Some of it's political, some pettiness, some protection of position. It's not always intentional, often just a careless loss of track in the shuffle of fifty other ideas. Just remember that we never took all our parents', teachers', president's or boss's ideas, either. So live with it and keep advising and giving suggestions. Remember most ace pilots were shot down several times, too. They won their medals going back up again!

Chapter 4

The Little Things... That Mean a Lot

Most bosses like and dislike the same things, you might be surprised to know —and a lot of them are little things.

I was in a truck on my way to a construction job once, for example, along with two foremen and five workers. We had to ride through a lot of fences to get where we were going, which also meant a lot of gates. Whenever we came to a gate, one worker eager to get to work, would jump out first and fast and open it. All of the others were getting paid just the same, but their whole objective was not to move off that seat unless they were commanded or ordered to. Little things like this score big with bosses.

A nice midtown church, on the other hand, hired three young men to redecorate the chapel. They were skilled painters and did a fine job for a fair price. So why didn't the boss (the minister) hire them for the other remodeling that needed attention on the premises? The reason was just a little thing—there was a handsome grand piano in the chapel and one of the painters was a pianist. Once or twice during the job he sat down at the piano bench in his painting clothes and played. He didn't hurt the piano and he wasn't cheating on his time because the job was contracted for a set price. But the boss heard about it and didn't like it. If the fellow had asked permission it would have been okay, but he didn't, so he was taking liberties with someone else's property. A little thing maybe, but it cut them out of a lot of work.

I've listened to and logged "the little things" from a lot of bosses over the years, and I'd like to share them with you here. These usually only come to light after a problem has developed or a job is lost. Now is a much better time to become aware of and avoid them.

Surprises—even good ones

Most bosses don't like to be surprised, even with good news. For instance, the division head of a company I was doing some work for once, invited an up-and-coming young project manager to accompany him to a meeting of the executive committee, to report on the progress of a job. This junior manager had just discovered that an error had been made in the cost projections for the job, which would mean an unexpected profit for the company of $20,000. He decided to save the big surprise for the meeting, where he could spring it himself and share in the glory that would surely come forth.

Unfortunately, the executive committee was not impressed. They were happy to have the extra $20,000, of course, but deeply concerned that an error of that magnitude had been made in the planning. The division manager, caught unawares, was totally unprepared to offer any kind of explanation for this major mistake on the part of his engineers. He emerged from the meeting looking bad, and feeling mighty unkindly toward his project manager.

Like any boss, this manager would rather have been informed of a thing like this in advance, so he could assess the impact on his department and decide how to handle it. Even if it was a serious problem, the fact that he was aware of it, had done the necessary research, and was taking steps to prevent a recurrence would have made him look much better in the eyes of the executive committee. By keeping him in the dark, his junior manager did him a real disservice, and didn't do anything to further his own career either. He wasn't in a position to judge where and how such information should be disclosed, and didn't understand the ramifications his "surprise" would have.

If it's not smart to spring good surprises on your boss, it's much worse when the news is not good. When something we're in charge of is going badly, for example, we often try to cover it up until we can get it fixed. Things like this can blow up in a big way if the problems come to light before we're ready to talk to the boss about them. The smart way to handle situations like this is to be totally up front, and let your boss know where things stand all the time. He or she may not like hearing about the problems on a project, but they'd surely rather find out about them while they're still small and solvable, than after they've gotten out of hand.

The least favorite surprise

Common courtesy, never mind ethics and good job politics, dictates some advance warning of upcoming events that will affect your availability.

Very few absences are real surprises or spur of the moment things. We usually know they are coming, but too often, in dread of the boss's wrath, hold off the bad news until we have to come out with it, usually at the last minute. If you sense or see it coming, be fair, polite, and considerate, give the boss some lead time. When an absence is planned for ahead of time much of the shock and irritation is defused. When it comes to giving notice, an hour is better than a few minutes, a day ahead is better than an hour, a week is better than a day, and if you can manage to anticipate a month ahead, the repercussions will be milder yet.

One of the surprises bosses like least is the sudden discovery that you're not going to be there when they were counting on you.

How far ahead should you let the boss know that...

You're leaving the job... 1 month to 2 weeks.

You want a certain day off... 2 weeks.

When you'd like to take your vacation... 6 months ahead.

You're pregnant... at least four months before the big day.

You've been called for jury duty... the minute you know.

You plan elective surgery... the longer it will keep you out, the sooner he should know.

You have to go to a funeral... as soon as you know.

Your own funeral... while your body is still warm.

Excuses

Your boss gets promoted and paid according to *how much* he or she can get accomplished, just like you and me. So no boss can be successful without subordinates who know how to get things done. When your boss assigns a task or project to you, he's counting on you to accomplish it.

None of us have a perfect batting average. We all occasionally strike out or fail to get the runs needed to win the game. What the boss needs, however, is someone he can count on to get results consistently. In the big leagues, getting a hit one out of three times at bat is a pretty good average. In business, we have to do better than that, but the principle is the same.

What would you think of a player who didn't get a hit very often, but always had a good excuse for it? "The sun was in my eyes." "That was a wicked puff of wind." "This new bat just isn't working for me." "That pitcher was throwing illegal pitches," etc. Would you expect the manager to keep using this guy? We really don't want to keep hearing why he didn't get a hit, do we? We just want to see him hit a reasonable percentage of the time.

Likewise, in your job, you want to be good enough (hit often enough) that your superiors are pleased with your performance, and don't overdo the excuses when you don't. When we dwell too much on the reasons we can't do things, we get caught up in negative thinking, and condition ourselves to expect less than optimum results. Expect to do well, and go out and do it. Then you'll be delivering what your boss really wants—results, not excuses.

After-you-get-there grooming

Many employees get up late, dash down to the office/shop/or whatever, check in by eight, and then use 30 or 40 of the boss's minutes to make themselves presentable: comb or restyle their hair, polish their shoes or their nails, put on makeup and earrings, etc., etc. Even models get beautiful on their own time.

Personal calls at work

(Or how to make the boss see red.) You can't cut off your personal life entirely when you work, but you can keep personal communications to a minimum. Personal calls made on company time will never be popular with bosses. We all know what these are—calls made to iron out family problems, advance romances, set up fishing trips, apply for loans, etc. Even if you aren't busy at the time and the calls are all local, using the company phone to tend to your personal affairs is a no-no. Emergencies and real necessities are okay and usually understood, but taking care of all your personal affairs on the company's time and phone system will do nothing to advance your popularity. Sneaking personal long distance calls onto the boss's phone bill is job suicide. Even when bosses don't mention this, *they're aware of it*, and they watch for it. 800 numbers and Watts lines aren't free as most people imagine. Using an 800 number to make personal calls to or from the workplace is no different than a regular long distance call—the boss is paying for every one.

On making yourself at home... at work

When you've cleaned up offices, schools, stores, banks, and all kinds of other business buildings as I have for more than 35 years as a pro cleaner, you can't help but notice the slow but steady migration of the home place to the workplace. We kind of absorb the feeling as time goes on that we own our little corner where we work, and so we bring photographs, pictures, posters, banners, trophies, plaques, and all kinds of other ornaments and decorations, as well as souvenirs, plants, cups, caps, clocks, and furniture. Some desks and areas are so full of knickknacks and coffee warmers, etc., that even dusting is practically impossible.

Even bosses enjoy a little reflection of your home, family, and hobbies at work, but they don't want a life-size, wide-screen view of it. Neither your china duck collection nor the group portrait of all your Chihuahuas will do anything to build confidence in the accounting firm you work for, and too much of this sort of stuff around could be taken as a signal that you'd like to be somewhere else.

In my own personal life I love "down home" decorating and family-oriented decorations, but as a boss and owner of offices I have to consider—for the good of all of us—a few other factors besides family:

1. **Safety:** A lot of this stuff creates hazards such as fire, falling over it, the chance of getting cut or shocked, etc.
2. **Security:** Nice things are the first to get broken or stolen.
3. **The cost of cleaning:** A "homey" office can take twice as long to clean, and if there are 10 or 100 offices...
4. **The distraction factor:** For you and others—they ask what it is, you have to stop to explain, etc.

Leaving the lights on, etc.

A husband and wife team who owned a small British publishing company were snorting fire as they drove me to their cottage in Wales once. It seemed that an employee of theirs (who scarcely turned on the heat all winter in her own home) went to the office, turned the heat up full blast, and then left doors and windows open all over. I've heard plenty of other bosses express the same frustrations with employees' lack of concern for the cost of heat, lights, air conditioning, water, etc. at the workplace. Somehow a lot of people have the idea that utilities must be free here. Bosses know it's not so because they have to pay all those bills. So they can't help noticing who left the water or the copier running.

Lack of concern for company assets

One of my employees and I were parked side by side talking and a cat ran up the side of the car. "Get off, you dumb critter" I said, "you'll scratch the car." "Oh that's okay," my employee said (forgetting who he was talking to), "it's a company car." Watch someone break a bat at a ball game—if it belongs to the boss or the ball club it's funny; if it's their own personal bat it's a cussing and weeping disaster.

Here's a few more common reflections of the attitude "it's the company's or the government's, so who cares":

- Leaving the company cars/tools out in the weather, while yours are carefully put away.
- Gunning vehicles, or treating them like all-terrain vehicles when they aren't.
- Taking a whole handful of napkins instead of what you need.

- Taking chances with the company computer that you never would with your own.
- Throwing away slightly soiled, wrinkled, or used things because there is a whole new box of them handy.
- Squeezing in a few personal repair items along with the company's.

Going wild when the workplace is paying

The boss or the company always seems to have a lot more money than we do, so when the company is paying, it's a clear signal to live high on the hog. Ever notice how:

- When the boss is buying at a restaurant, our taste jumps from hamburger to prime rib? The boss notices too.
- Our own choice of motel is Super 8 or Motel 6, but when the company is paying, we want a Marriott suite.
- At the car rental counter, there's no such thing as a compact "for company use."
- On the plane or train, "coach" or budget class is always fine with us, unless, again, the company is paying.
- Gifts and tips to others are always bigger if it's going to be charged to the boss.

Amazing, isn't it, how tastes can vary according to who's footing the bill.

The attitude and practice that'll get you the best press here is: "When the boss is paying I'll rent, eat, drive, sleep, and dress the same as on my own money."

Helping yourself to company facilities

One night at 10:30 p.m. (we close at 5:00) I was passing my corporate office and saw a light. When I went in I found one of my manager's sons, age 21, doing his college homework on my computer, using my paper and photocopier. His girl friend was slouched on the couch gobbling up my popcorn.

When I asked him what he was doing, he said, "Well, it was just sitting here and you have lots of computers and I don't have any."

Bosses don't like this kind of attitude at all. Asking special permission to use company property once in a while is one thing. Asking for it often is pushing it, and helping yourself without asking is job suicide. But access always seems to encourage excess—you let an employee park or leave a car on the company lot, and pretty soon a second car with a boat trailer is there. Employees use my place and space to store Christmas presents, and to do messy projects they wouldn't sully their own garage or cellar with.

Bosses generally do own more tools, vehicles, and equipment than most people, and I've noticed an attitude that once you work for a company or boss their tools and supplies are yours, to use any place or way that you please.

I've always been generous with vehicles, for example, and I usually leave the keys right in my company car. One night I came back to the office at 8:30 and ALL of the company cars were gone, my own personal company car included. "Taking the general's jeep, too" as I described it the next morning, was not only wrong but dumb. It turned out that four of those seven missing vehicles were off on personal errands that night—church activities, transporting a couch or a crib, etc.—all important, of course. And as the borrowers involved said, "How else could we have moved it? We don't have a truck but you do."

Vacuums, rug shampooers, ladders, tables, and chairs disappear overnight regularly, too. First it's the shampooer, then the shampoo, then some garbage bags or cleaning cloths, after all, the boss has cases of them. So goes the gradual evolution of false ownership, until you have a $50,000-a-year executive risking his job for 3 rolls (worth all of $1.09) of toilet paper "borrowed" from the boss.

Likewise, I see constantly where companies at their expense provide meals and fruit, etc. for employees, many of whom soon begin to load up a few extras to "take home to the kids."

There is magic in "Getting permission!"

No personal sales pitches, please

Bosses don't like employees using their organizations (phone, personal contacts, mail service, etc.) for personal crusades or campaigns, whether it's selling insurance or championing causes, however worthwhile.

I can't tell you how many times during work hours I've found my people preaching the gospel, selling cosmetics, setting up an Avon or Amway client, or holding a rally for a favorite politician. The workplace isn't a congregation conveniently assembled for you to address. We all have our favorite causes, we all want to right some wrong in the world or the neighborhood. But work isn't the place to do it. This doesn't just take time away from your work—it creates the impression that the

boss too is pushing the cause or product in question. Using your position, your time on the job, or the company bulletin board or copier to rouse your fellow workers will cause plenty of problems for you.

This includes, meritorious as they may be in themselves, campaigns for weight loss, stopping smoking, etc. I've seen whole sections of my operation affected by someone on a public diet, for example. It takes an hour of everyone's time and 20 listeners to review current poundage and what they ate to accomplish it, etc. Then recipes and menus have to be copied and passed around. (The company provides all the paper and copies, of course.)

Making idleness too obvious

Even if you aren't busy on the job sometimes, carrying a big pile of schoolbooks, the latest hot paperback novel, or that half-knitted sweater to the job with you gives a bad impression.

Most people got to be bosses by hustling. So secretly or not so secretly, they expect everyone to hop and jump and run as fast as they do. Idleness—standing around, drowsing, chit-chatting about obviously personal matters—is a real red flag to bosses. They read it as:

1. You're lazy.
2. You don't have enough to do.
3. You're bored.
4. You don't like your work.

Being busy, or even too busy, on a job is a blessing. You never want to seem slow or idle, even if it means getting out of sight or doing push-ups. If you're caught staring into space even once it gives you a big black mark. Bosses HATE to see idleness, any time or place, in any situation. It's kind of like going into a store to pay for something, having the clerk take your money, then stand there and never give you the item. That's exactly how the boss feels when you stop working or just stand around. The boss is giving you money and getting nothing back. A bad deal!

I once heard a boss ask another boss about a new employee: "Is he steady?" "Steady!" exclaimed the second boss, "Why he's motionless!" Bosses find briskness—and even people who occasionally break into a run—irresistible.

So be prepared:

1. First, be sure you know **everything** you need to do on your job.
2. ASK, find out what the boss wants you to do, give him or her the first benefit of any free time you have.
3. Make your own list for "When I get some spare time."

Some Do's

Clean
Dejunk
File
Hustle new business on the phone
Update
Create that badly needed form
Service and maintain tools and equipment
Practice
Train yourself
Help a co-worker
Work ahead

Some Don'ts

Stand around
Lay down
Doze or sleep
Tinker
Groom yourself
Disappear
Take longer breaks
Have an extended conversation with a customer or co-worker
Do personal reading (books, magazines, etc.)
Call your friends or folks
Eat on the job
Put your feet on the desk

Just don't spring it on them

Most of us, if we know our job as well as we should, can and will anticipate spare or vacant time coming. Never wait until it arrives and wander into the boss and tell her right then, that you're all caught up, is there anything you can do? Bosses don't like this kind of timing.

It's so sudden, they're unprepared, so they have to search frantically for something worthwhile, intelligent, and well timed for you to do. (Which is tough to come up with in a minute or two.)

So go with the same approach a day or two before. "Boss, I'll about be caught up, I'm going to have the rest of the week available and want to keep busy. Let me know what special projects, or extra, or more work I can do." They'll love you, it gives them time to outline some things, instead of a five-minutes-notice panic!

Is the boss looking?

This is an age-old trick that only tricks the trickster, the old "when the cat's away, the mice will play." We tried it when parents were out of sight, the teacher was out of the room, the coach's or the sergeant's back was turned. And now when the boss is out of the office or out of town we slack off a little, or a lot. It's almost a game of "catch me if you can." In my day it was called horsing around or skipping out, and it seemed like all the "big boys" did it. They cut laps on the ball field, let the new worker lift more sacks or fill out more forms.

I remember back when a local farmer hired the high school boys to truck spuds. He was a good boss and paid well. Yet as soon as they unloaded a truckload in the spud cellar, while they were there out of sight of the field where the boss was, the crew would lounge, pinch butts, and lay around to what they figured was the limit, then return for another load. They figured it was cool to cut work time. It wasn't—it was just dishonest and sneaky.

One day the boss was working quietly in the other end of the cellar when they came in, and he stood right behind them for ten minutes as they made fun of him and loafed while he paid them a nice salary. Suddenly one kid saw him and in seconds they all scrambled guiltily toward the potato bins. The boss went up to the truck and removed the keys from it and without a word, just pointed down the road. They were ashamed and humiliated and out of work, now, too!

Don't include this trick in your work habits, folks. Bosses know or always find out about it, whether they're in or out of sight of what you're doing. It takes a real scumball to take someone's money and trust, and then cheat him.

Failing to arrive dressed and ready to do some real damage

I hired three husky fourteen-year-olds (anxious to make some money) once to help me build some trails, lay cement, and pick rocks at my ranch. When they showed up, one didn't have a coat or hat, one didn't have gloves, and they all had on tennis shoes. "Are you guys here to work or play volleyball?" I asked them. "Work," they chorused. Well, they spent half their time digging small rocks out of their sneakers, picking burdocks off their clothes and gloves, going to the bathroom, shivering, checking with mom and arranging their rides home. I picked a lot more rock than they did, and loaded my side of the wagon twice—they were amazed that an "old man" could outdo all of them combined. "You guys didn't come to work, you came to twink," I told them. "Next time I want boots, gloves, goggles, and domestic silence (no advice from Mother)." They did it, and their productivity tripled.

Working at home

Bosses don't like "work done at home" when there's an office with regular office hours. "I'm taking my calls at home," or "I'm going to take this all home and really dig into it and get to the bottom of it." In most cases, you are the only one this really suits—it's expensive and inconvenient for everyone else, and doesn't give a businesslike impression even when the boss does it.

Gum chewing

"Ill bred—enough said." (As a professional cleaner of workplaces I could also note what a hard- or impossible-to-remove mess "used gum" makes of wastebaskets, floors, and parking areas!)

Smoking

Is a plague to bosses. It really costs them. It raises the cost of their health insurance, adds greatly to the cost of cleaning and maintaining the building, injures furnishings and fixtures, and uses up a lot of energy keeping the air quality acceptable for the other nonsmoking employees. I won't hire a smoker—I might like what they could do for me, they might even be family or friends, but I just won't have the habit around my workplace. I'm not the only boss who feels this way.

Grub gripes

America's greatest passion and favorite pastime—is it TV, sports, cars, sex... or apple pie? Now you're talking—it's FOOD. Food is everywhere, all the time. We can't watch a ballgame, drive across town, fly anywhere, have a meeting, or even do a few hours of work without food! We must be nibbling, munching, chewing, smacking, slurping, and rattling food around constantly, no matter what we're doing. Despite the fact that most of us are overfed and overweight.

And what a weight this is on the workplace! Three square meals (two at home, one at work) don't seem to cut it. We have to eat around the clock and really complicate our lives on the job. No boss likes it when one of her people carries in a huge "Giant Gulp" container of cola or coffee and sets it right next to a $10,000 computer. Or sips and slurps nonstop while talking. Or spills and drops and leaves food and drink all over the desk and the work and the floor. Always having to put down a snack or a mug to handle a call or assist a customer is genuinely gross behavior. As is breathing burrito breath on them or smiling hello with taco chip fragments in your teeth. Then, too, when we eat and drink constantly, we're constantly wiping our hands and mouth and running to the restroom to reapply or recycle lipstick. Or sending someone out (what a timewaster, if not an insult!) to fetch sandwiches and salads and other goodies. The aftermath of food fallout lays grotesquely around. The wrappers and bags and part packages of stuff that no one knows whether is old enough to chuck yet, and the leftovers attract all kinds of insects as well as rats and mice.

There's a time to eat and drink, and it isn't all the time. Shoveling donuts, mints, and other munchies in your mouth nonstop is out of place in a classy workplace!

Another pet peeve

Workers who spend their entire lunch hour doing personal stuff, then bring their lunch back to the office and eat it on company time, leaving a big mess and a bad impression.

Bad language

What you say and how you say it is a very large part of the company's image, in the eyes and ears of clients and customers. Vulgar language is out—even bosses who use it don't like it. They might be foul-mouthed themselves, but they don't want to hear it from you. After 35 years in business I've yet to find a place where profanity of any kind is welcome.

Likewise, those mindless little expressions we find ourselves repeating, like "Yeah" and "You know" will irritate both bosses and customers. And just as your fourth grade teacher told you, so will bad grammar, even from the mouth of a rough tough construction worker. Bad language of this kind throws your (and the company's) intelligence into question.

Regional flavor

As for that unique flair or flavor your voice may have as a result of where you were born and raised, it can be a plus or a minus, depending on the boss, the business, and the situation.

Some accents might give you an advantage as a head waiter, wine steward, or waltz teacher. And I know of at least one former Easterner who got her present job in the Midwest because she has a heavy New Jersey accent. The company she works for does credit and collections back East and they needed someone who could "speak the language." Their present collectors were getting nowhere at all calling with their genteel, polite, Midwestern voices.

When my cleaning company had the maintenance contract for the famous Sun Valley resort (which has a kind of Swiss Alpine flavor), I remember how charming it was at first to have a young man or woman actually from Switzerland work there, complete with that Nordic accent. Yet a year or two later when a whole troupe of them worked there, it was no big thing. It had lost its impact.

A little "foreign charm" is great anywhere it thrills the natives... or the customers. A few "Howdy Ma'ams" and "Y'all come backs" can go a long way in the right situation. Just remember that "cute" gets old anywhere eventually, so don't lay on your charm too thick or too fast. If it fits, fine, but just don't fake it. Bosses (like most everyone) hate phonies. If you're from out of town, across the country or across the ocean, a real cowboy or a real Carolinian, or a former Miss Dangerous Curve, it won't carry you at work indefinitely. So go easy... pardner.

Radios blasting while you work

I know we all secretly feel we're giving others a treat when we bombard them with our taste in music, but radios blaring while you work run a good risk of offending others as well as distracting them, especially somewhere like an office where people are doing mental work.

A noisy radio can be a nuisance almost anywhere, though. On our way home from a long trip one evening, my wife and I stopped at an upscale restaurant in town for supper. One of the cooks had his radio set up in the back playing some of the loudest and most annoying music I ever heard. When the waitress came I offered her a $10 tip to please turn off the radio. When she went and told the chef about it he gave a surly answer and turned it up. It was a nice restaurant owned by nice people who had just gone home. Needless to say it was the last time I ever went there or took any of my people there or recommended it to anyone.

The silent tune-in, via headphones, isn't really any better. Wearing and working with a headset tells a boss you aren't very interested in the job, you care little about safety, or hearing or hearkening to the words or needs of others.

While you are tuning in, others are usually tuning you out!

Leaving your co-workers stranded when they're busy

This happens a lot. In stores, for example, someone goes to the back for something and doesn't come back for fifteen minutes (because "they couldn't find it" or some other lame excuse). Meanwhile the person up front is handling crowds of people that are getting madder by the minute because the service is so slow.

Taking a break at the busiest time of the day

Not a good idea, because it makes it look as if you're oblivious or inconsiderate, or you can't handle pressure so you have to get away.

Don't take your break at a busy time, even if it's scheduled. Let things ease off before you ease out. Both the boss and your co-workers and clients will notice and appreciate it!

Gabbing to co-workers while customers wait/grumble

Another pet peeve of my daughter, who hires a lot of young people. "I've had employees start to tell me stories right while I'm talking to or waiting on a customer. You don't turn to them and say hush up right in front of people, but you're tempted to. I usually assign

them a job." (If you've been getting a lot of little "emergency" jobs lately, take heed!)

Visiting, gabbing, blabbing, gossiping, chatting while working is one of the biggest irritants for bosses. Even when people think they're working full steam ahead, constant conversation misdirects thoughts and concentration and costs bosses billions of dollars a year. They don't like it!

The old toilet "stall"

When you gotta go, you gotta go—but using a big part of the workday to redo makeup, read in the restroom, pick pimples, adjust clothes, etc., is noticed and makes bosses nervous.

Not being willing to go the extra five

Bosses do expect a little extra time once in a while—such as being willing to stay an extra five or ten minutes when you're really needed, or to finish up something.

Another daughter of mine had a young man working in her ice cream parlor in Alaska who set his digital watch to go off at the end of his shift. He could be right in the middle of serving a double-dip ice cream cone, but when it rang at 5:00 p.m. he'd drop the scoop in the bucket, say "I'm off," and leave. The customer left holding the one scoop of his two-scoop order would freak out!

Piggy parking

If you work in a place that deals with the public, especially, you never want to take the closest and best spots for your vehicle. Leave them for the customers, the elderly, those with more kids or heavier bags. People (even bosses) resent those who take the best or closest spot, even if they did get there first! Never take that place "right in front of the door," and tell your friends the same—bosses will notice and appreciate it.

Like you, I'm not much of one for labeled parking places. I'm with those who believe that if someone's so important, they'll be there first anyway. However, "private label" parking is pretty sacred to some people. Even if your first impulse is to sneer, honor the name on it and move down a slot or two.

Mood swings

Since most bosses have to ride this roller coaster with their customers (and maybe at home, too), they don't need it with their employees. No boss wants to be sitting there wondering whether it's PMS, a family fight, an overdue car payment, or a hangover that's causing the sour face on someone. A boss just doesn't want or need the extra hassle. So no matter how bad things are or have been, at home or elsewhere, find your leveling agents on the way to work and use them. Don't unsettle the boss with erratic mood swings. For that matter, most bosses don't like

dancing and prancing on Friday afternoon any better than moping and groaning on Monday mornings. So remember to leave your personal problems at home and *level it!*

Bringing your scepter to work

Another good thing to leave at home is your ruling status. You may be the king or empress of your own little spread, you can demand anything or just snap your fingers and your kids or spouse leap to do your bidding. But at work you have to take orders, not give them, unless giving orders is what you're assigned to do. As an employee you're usually the server. You're not there to be served.

The expression "overqualified"

Don't ever use the expression "I'm overqualified" to a boss—bosses don't believe that anyone is overqualified to do honest work. We can all wash dishes or clean up dog doo when we have to or need to. Don't ever infer that you're overqualified for (too good for) a job, especially one you're applying for!

Snooping

Bosses hate it. There is, I agree, sometimes a fine line between interest and interference. But looking in drawers, reading stuff on other people's desks, and moving or handling things

that are no concern of yours is OUT if you want to stay in the boss's good graces.

Some trying "prying:"

- Opening others' mail.
- Reading papers directed to someone else (before they even have a chance to).
- Slowing down to catch passing conversations.
- Asking questions that are none of your business.

Constantly asking how much the boss makes

If the company is privately held, don't be forever trying to find out how much the boss or the company makes. You may think you have a right to know; you can be sure your boss thinks he has a right to keep it his business. I know it will bug you to death to see all that money coming in compared to your paltry sum, but remember all bosses pay hundreds of expenses, including ones *you've* made necessary, that you never know about. They take all the risk and often go without when you are paid. The boss doesn't, or shouldn't, snoop into your private finances and you shouldn't snoop into his. The bottom line is that the boss's income is off limits. If you just can't stand not knowing, you need to go start the same kind of business yourself, then you'll know and I'll bet you'll be surprised!

Snow jobs

Risky! What snow the boss doesn't see through, melts quickly. Besides, most bosses have used all of your clever tricks of flattery themselves somewhere along the line, so they aren't fooled or impressed, only irritated.

Setting your boss up to help you do something you could easily do yourself, for example, in an attempt to get points or make

them look good, is just going to make *you* look like a jerk when she sees through it. Same goes for pretending to be interested in a boss's undertaking or event, when you aren't. Giving faked "roll on the floor in delight" responses to what the boss likes. Being there early just on the days the boss is in town, or timing your showups to his stop-ins. Joining his or her church when you don't care anything about it. Over-complimenting his or her looks, abilities, or success. Hanging a picture of his hometown high school team in your office. Or trying to talk enthusiastically about his garden or golf game when you know little or nothing about it. All of the above means just a wet blanket to the boss. It's self-production that impresses him or her, not self-promotion.

A longtime employee of mine has used a few snow jobs on me, but no amount of encouragement on my part has ever managed to make her change her fishing style from bait to flies. I think she's dumb for it, but I sure have to respect her honesty!

"Calling in sick"

Once not long ago, when this country was young and strong, if you were sick you not only didn't get paid, you had to find a way to replace yourself. Then business went on to make concessions for the frailties of the human body, providing paid time off for when you were really sick. Now most employees see sick leave as simply additional paid days off. And even if they're not sick, they'll use sick leave time to go on vacation, go fishing, or go shopping—because they see these days as fully owed to them, "their right." So they plan to be sick, and "calling in sick" is even part of our everyday language!

Calling in sick on holidays or the day of the big game is common now. "Everybody is doing it, so why shouldn't I do it?" You can, but it's dishonest, and bosses despise dishonesty. They always find out and they get "sick" of it!

Gossip

Hawaiians have the perfect word for this practice: *Holoholo oleo* .

"Holoholo" means to wander around aimlessly, and "oleo" means to speak. This makes it clear why we aren't a bit impressive when we're gossiping.

If you carry or transfer any gossip (unproven information and rumors), you are a rag mag on the hoof and a reckless polluter of the boss's backyard. So serious is gossip that the Lord included it in the big ten ("Thou shalt not bear false witness") right along with "Thou shalt not kill." Gossip isn't all that different. After all, when you kill someone you cause a separation of their spirit and body, and when you gossip about someone you often separate them from their reputation, which can be about as bad as being dead!

Don't spike your lunch at work with gossip. Remember that listening to it is as bad as spreading it. Like the AIDS virus, even if you didn't start it, if you carry it you're just as dangerous.

Gossiping isn't just a waste of time. It's a high-risk pastime. All during your career, remember that loose words and actions don't go in the trash where they belong, they go in the boss's file cabinet. He or she doesn't seek them out, he doesn't have to. Your colleagues and the public do their police job well and will air it all, live or recorded, sometime when the boss is listening or watching. Idle chatter during coffee breaks, for example, has undone a lot of "breaks" employees might have gotten. You might keep this in mind before a slip of the lips or hips.

The Robin Hood hassle

No boss needs it, nor do you want the consequences of robbing "the rich" (the boss) to feed "the poor " (you). The boss always seems to have plenty, a lot more than you, and too often greed germinates into the right to " borrow" or take a little from the company—pens, paper, photocopies, books, work gloves, food, a tool or two, etc. No real dishonesty, just a few little extra things no one will miss.

If you are a workplace thief, don't count on disappearing into Sherwood Forest. What starts as tiny always turns into tonnage. One mountain states area executive once told me his company "budgeted" $17,000 a *day* for thievery (most of it within the company). It shouldn't be tolerated, let alone budgeted for. It's a shameful reality, however. Don't ever be a part of it.

In more than 35 years of running a large company I've dealt with my share of thieves, including people we had a lot of faith and confidence in, and people we gave a good job to when no one else would hire them. One office manager we all boosted and admired embezzled $10,000 from us, and plenty of others have ripped the company off (for less than that, maybe, but still lots). Dishonesty

always leaves a trail. You don't have to hire a detective to uncover it, it just kind of emerges, always at the wrong time for the thief. Piles of company credit card slips pass my desk regularly, for example. Yet when a pair of 14" snow tires shows up on one (none of our company vehicles take that size tire), I know immediately that one of my managers has charged his wife's tires to us. Or I'll be visiting a friend in another town and he'll mention a job he paid for that we didn't finish. I'll check the company job sheet—nothing—get my friend's check number and call the bank, and find the check deposited in my manager's personal account. He stole company money.

Another time I did a job with one of my top managers, someone I trusted completely. We were painting a utility pole and while he was wrestling around at the top his wallet slipped out. It fell twenty feet and the contents spilled out all over the ground, right in front of my face. There was a $150 check from one of our old customers (one we hadn't seen much of recently) for a rug cleaning job, made out to him personally. He never knew I knew... that he was a thief.

If you steal, never think you got away with it just because the boss might not say anything right away. I just destroyed (in an act of kindness) a large 25-year-old confidential file of all the reports and documentation of employees who stole from me. Some of them were good friends and highly valued employees. None of them knew I knew, but dishonesty sends up flares and people can't wait to report it. Some of these I prosecuted, but most I didn't have to. Between my watching and limiting the trust I placed in them after that, and their own lack of respect for themselves, they just "stole" away.

Stealing either time or property from your boss is cholesterol that quietly and insidiously builds up in your employment artery. If you steal, in time you'll get caught by the boss, or by yourself. Four years after one secretary worked in our office we received several huge sheets of stamps in the mail, along with an apology, from a repentant young woman who found she couldn't live with what she did to those who trusted her.

Whether the boss ever knows anything about it or not, *you* know, and you have to live with that knowledge. Coming to work every day knowing full well that you are robbing someone who is providing you with a job to feed yourself and your family is going to make you feel pretty low life. It will file an edge off of you that dulls your personality and job performance. No calculator, computer accessory, or packet of pens is worth that.

Getting involved with the boss's wife or husband

Here's a flashing caution light for sure. Bosses and owners are more likely than the average worker to have a spouse. He or she may even work right with or around you. Consider the fact that 60% of all marriages ultimately fail, and at least 75% are a little uneasy, and add to that the ever-present strain of being in charge, and you have a pretty fragile situation. The imagination of a spouse can drum up some pretty farfetched jealousies. If the boss even mentions an employee (especially one of the opposite sex) in a tone of praise, little red flags go up immediately. Even if you are devoted to the death to the boss and do your job in an unfailingly whiz-bang way, their spouse may squint at you even if you're making their mate a million.

Bosses are sensitive about your communicating directly with their spouse, especially concerning the job or works in progress. The best summary here is the old saying: "You can't serve two masters." There is wisdom and safety in sharing and discussing things only with your direct boss, and taking only her advice and orders. Be polite, acknowledging, and helpful to the spouse, but always channel things through, answer to, and get permission from, your boss, not their "better half."

Getting a mile and taking inches more

Often a boss will come through with a surprise, a raise, a generous offer, a day off, a new tool, an upgrade of some kind which delights us to no end. Yet something inside our greedy little head says: "Gee, she's on a roll, and gave us all this, maybe she'd go for another one, or at least a little bit more." In other words, they give us a new car and we ask if it has cruise control, or "Is it full of gas?" We get a $15,000 perk but we just have to eke out that $15 tank of gas. Most bosses hate this.

One location where I ran my cleaning operations for a while was way up in the mountains of Idaho, far from most of my workers' homes. Many of them would try to spend some weekends at home, and I knew it.

So even though Friday was usually a heavy day for us, I'd set things up so we could start earlier and then they could take off for home by three p.m. instead of six. They were thrilled and thanked me profusely, but after they had a chance to think about it they started easing into my office and asking "Well Don, what if we came in an hour earlier yet and then left by noon?" I was a little irritated, but I okayed it, and within a day a proposal was presented for leaving by Thursday night! Before long we were working our way toward Thursday noon, and some even rationalized all the way back to noon Wednesday. It wasn't just one or two of my workers, they all did it. It got so that my wife and I would place bets on them from the moment they announced they were going home for the weekend.

This is something bosses see a lot. If they give one hour or two free, the help is soon pressing for three and four and then five.... Likewise, employees ask to borrow the company truck for a day—"Okay"—inevitably they ask to keep it longer and ask for it more often. Bosses really turn off on things like this.

Bosses hate to be leaned on for exceptions. They always feel good about granting something special that really helps you, most bosses are willing to do this and they feel good about it. They're happy to give some inches when they can, but abuse the privilege and keep angling and levering for more or as much as you can possibly get, and they'll have just the opposite reaction.

Putting in overtime the boss didn't ask for

If you're paid by the hour it's always a good idea to ask the boss about extra hours before working them. In most cases the boss will agree, but if you'll be running into overtime rate he or she will naturally want to make sure it's not only useful but necessary.

You don't want to be like the tour guide whose shift started at 8:00 a.m. He couldn't sleep, so he decided to come in at 5:00 a.m. instead!

Bosses are always extra sensitive to how high-priced hours are spent. One of my daughters, for example, had an employee in her clothing store who wanted to put in some extra time. So she told the woman to start tagging shirts. She tagged four shirts and then jammed the tag gun, and instead of asking for help she spent the rest of the time trying to fix it. She didn't succeed. So her boss had to pay for a ruined tag gun as well as three wasted hours of overtime.

Running a second job on your job

Some of my janitors once were taking longer than they should have to clean a routine area. I watched them one night and found that as they cleaned past pay phones or upholstered furniture, they were rummaging around for left-behind cash—taking all the cushions off the couch, etc., not to clean but to feel for money. I've seen other pro cleaners interrupt their routine to collect pop cans, salvage stuff out of dumpsters, etc. Private enterprise is fine. Just keep it off the job and on your own time.

The same goes for pursuing hobbies, such as getting your pilot's license, on the company's time and at the company's expense. It's great to have a collection of any kind going, for instance, but practicing it at the job at the expense of the job "doesn't work." I knew a young man who collected autographs, who was forever interrupting sales and customer service at the TV station where he worked to get autographs. One day he found himself begging for the most important autograph of all—his boss's signature on his check.

The job you're at now may be a second job, or even one of several that you have. Just bear in mind that no boss likes to be a second fiddle or a hand-me-down or to get the leftovers. So keep your mouth shut about one job while you're on the other, and keep a clean separation between the two—don't wear your lab coat to your library job.

There's no way a second job—no matter how small—won't interfere with your first. So choose, and choose carefully.

Looking down your nose at the locals

Never bad-mouth the town or community that's providing your job. It's signing your name on the ungrateful list to moan and complain about how much it costs to live, eat, park, or buy things there. You're generally there by choice (yours), because you can make more money and have more advantages than you could back home. Things might be higher, hotter, or less hospitable here than home, but you'd be wise to keep quiet about it. Neither the boss nor the townfolks appreciate whiners.

Getting bent because the boss calls you at home

We couldn't count the times we or our family and friends have called the workplace for personal reasons. So we should surely forgive the boss for an invasion of our personal space every once in a while.

Your connections with the boss and the workplace on your "off" time will depend a lot on your exact situation and setup, of course—whether you're salaried, hourly, or contract labor. Emergencies, changes of plans or weather, travel schedule cancellations, etc. can all happen "after hours," and in order to have order when worktime rolls around, an advance call or contact is often both necessary and welcome. Or your boss may be on a business trip somewhere (in a different time zone maybe) and need your help or advice. Some invasions of privacy can be lifesavers, and others just a big help. If the boss calls you at home to inform you that a shipment came in late, for instance, so we're all going to be unloading and processing stuff outside tomorrow, you'll be forewarned to wear sneakers and Levis instead of a suit and high heels. Or a message to stop on the way in to pick up something could save an extra trip for you both.

Bosses, on the other hand, who call you at bedtime or mealtime to spend an hour going over business that could just as well be done any other time at work, are out of bounds.

Playing the mule

You can rate yourself right in with those balky animals here by deliberately or unconsciously not doing an assignment, or not doing it the way the boss wants it done. This usually comes about because we don't agree that something should be done, or with how he or she wants to do it. The best advice I can give you here is that the boss *is* the boss. Do what they've asked for, and expect. Otherwise the person who's going to end up getting "kicked" is you.

Criticizing the boss or the company

The most common error employees make! True, we all have a right to our opinion, but that doesn't mean it's always a wise idea to announce it. Plenty of bosses are deserving of criticism, but if it isn't your specific assignment to do so I'd keep it to myself. The reason is simple—people will rarely take advice if they haven't asked for it, so unsolicited criticism will do little or no good. No one likes being criticized, and bosses are no different from the rest of us when it comes to this. You have nothing to gain and everything to lose. Criticism shared with third parties always gets back to the boss, *always.* Even your best friend who happens to work for the same person will tell. They won't be able to resist sharing your secret slices at the boss, especially those really clever ones, with someone, and that will eventually mean the boss. Bosses don't have to make an effort to find out who's saying what. Loyal (and for that matter plenty of disloyal) co-workers will be only too happy to report it.

Don't think you're safe going home to do your criticizing. Airing your gripes at home can be even worse than doing so in the workplace. A few years back I took all our top managers and their wives to Hawaii for the most important event of our business year, our annual company meeting. In the course of the trip several of the wives commented to me how happy they were to find out that the president of the company was actually human. Before this, one woman said, all she knew about him was what her husband came home and told her—old Aslett is tight, hardhearted, tough, thoughtless, and a real slave driver. So she and her family came to know the boss as a jerk, because her husband fed them all bad vibes and created a highly negative climate. Everything was "the rotten boss's" fault, and by now the family agreed and reinforced it. Once the wives met and spent some time with the boss, they came to realize that the real jerks might just be their husbands. The company's support on the home front picked up tremendously after this trip, and productivity did, too.

Listening to criticism of the hand that feeds you, by the way, is pretty close to being part of it. If you're in a group and hear criticism of the boss and don't refute it or remove yourself from the discussion, you become an endorser of the remarks. Finding something positive to say (even if you have to work a little to find something) is always a smart practice.

Second guessing

With bosshood or ownership comes platoons of would-be consultants, counselors, analysts, advisors, and inspectors. Let me advise you not to try and add yourself to this list. Bosses love suggestions and ideas, but when decisions are made they sure don't want any second guessers.

Second guessing is a questioning of the boss's competence. Not only does that burn him up, but second guessing always slows up progress, muddles direction, and encourages others to become second guesser trainees!

Bosses have the right to do with their money and business what they want, and you as a worker need to understand that. They don't tell you how to spend your money, and you should honor their right to use their own money and facilities as they wish. I know lots of bosses who use one profitable business to support another (losing) one, such as a horse farm. If they love the farm, the salary they pay the farm manager, the money they spend on hay, and the time they take away from the profitable business to visit the farm is their right and their business. Some bosses launch projects and programs that lose money, some waste their resources, some drink, some gamble, some donate all their profits to charity. Fine! It's theirs!

Those little business gifts

The workplace is always a tug of war for position and profits, and if you have a job that can influence what appears in dad's store or the boss's plant or office, you'll soon find salespeople offering you "incentives." "Buy a dozen of each and you get a free watch or transistor radio or jacket." Be careful—there's a fine line between promotion and taking on an obligation. I knew a telephone company boss whose policy was to refuse all free lunches, hats, pocketknives, etc., from vendors. Lots of his people, however, didn't refuse and often found themselves squirming in "deals" they really didn't want.

Taking employee discounts for granted

A lot of us think of it as our right to have an employee discount on anything the company produces or sells. Or that we should expect to be able to buy our tires, clothes, fuel, etc. through the company to get a better deal or discount. We feel we have a right to this, that it's automatically part of our pay, but it isn't.

Anything I'm asked to do... is my job

Most bosses have done every job in the place and deep in their hearts, they expect you to want to do the same. Bosses hate "That isn't my job" or "I don't know how." And they love "Yes, sir" or "You got, it Ma'am."

It's called *flexibility*.

Show that you care

Showing genuine concern for the boss's business whether you're at home, at work or away goes a long way with a good boss. Surprise him or her and call in from a trip or vacation sometime, asking if all is well.

Make those extra talents known

Most of us have any number of skills and abilities the boss doesn't know about. We can sing, dance, draw, tune a piano, play the guitar, set up stage lighting, do calligraphy, overhaul motors, climb the highest light pole, or catch escaped canaries quicker than anyone alive. "I'm a waitress now, but I ran a cash register once so I can easily fill in for the hostess who won't be able to come in Saturday." When the opportunity comes up to use one of your unknown talents for the boss or some company activity, be sure to volunteer. It'll gain you points, and may even gain you some new and interesting work assignments.

Bosses need to know the things you can do and the things you'd like to do. It's to a boss's advantage to fit you into a better slot, to make you more productive and happy. So make it easy for them. Mention in conversation or writing that you can do this or that. You may want to volunteer (offer to do a job you like, or that fits your talents, free for a while).

Your boss—get to know him or her

I've mentioned a lot of little things in this chapter that can put the boss into orbit (most bosses are fairly high strung anyway). I know you don't live to kowtow to a psychotic boss, but remember that what's real to them—silly or picky as it may seem to you—will have an effect on their behavior toward you. Lots of people joke about the odd or seemingly petty things that nibble at the nerves of their employer. But remember that a tiny rudder sets the course for a giant ship and journey.

I certainly haven't agreed with all the bosses I've had. I haven't seen eye to eye with all of them. But as long as I work for someone, I make a point of finding out what they like and don't like, what they want and don't want... and I give it to them.

Why is that a good idea? Because like all the rest of us, bosses live with irritations if they have to, but they'll rid themselves of them as soon as they can.

All bosses have certain things that really annoy them. Some of these are little, some big, some entirely reasonable and understandable, and some just plain quirky and peculiar to them. What don't I like, for example? Loud shoes or boots, too much perfume, and long fingernails. Someone gulping down Coke, coffee or M &M's while they're meeting with or talking to me. I hate any kind of disruptive, unnecessary noises, too: nervous whistling or tapping, ice chewing or rattling, constant wheezing, coughing, or sniffing, radios blaring away on the job. I don't like to see people dragging things instead of carrying them. And it infuriates me when people don't answer little children, or look over their heads, or ignore them when they're around. As does being shuffled off the phone for "call waiting"!

What little things irritate your boss? If I were you, I'd find out.

SLOTH
GREED
GREE

Chapter 5

Your Goals: Raises, Perks, and Promotions

As not only a boss but a writer for many years now, I like to boil big concepts and pages of important principles down to one or two lines and post them on the wall as signs. This way it's easy for those working for me to know what I like and what they have to do to please me, to get what they're working for, and more of it.

When we're looking for a job, for the right place to work, we all ask the same questions:

What is the job?

What do we do?

How much do we get paid?

Where can we advance to?

If those four questions are answered to our satisfaction, we go after the job. Once we're hired, we soon quit worrying about the first two questions and start concentrating on: How much can I get paid? and when and how do I advance to the top from here? Ironically, to get what we want we should really forget about the last two questions and concentrate on the first two: What is the job? and what do I do? If we find out and focus on these two things, raises and advancements will come by themselves, often so fast you won't believe it.

In other words, good work and high performance is the answer. But most people spend most of their time concentrating on other issues, such as seniority, security, position, perks, and benefits. I find it interesting that if you ask people what they want to earn and exactly what they're aspiring to, most of them can't answer either of these questions.

"How much do you want to earn?" "Well, all I can." That's a pretty dumb answer because "all you can" depends entirely on you, not the boss.

Likewise, when I say "What is 'the top' for you?" I hear things like: "Well, ah... the highest position." A lot of people think a bigger job means one where you get more pay for less work—whereas the exact opposite is true. A better job only means raising your output or the amount and quality of work that you do.

I've never seen people who come to a job with money, power, and position as their main purpose ever become great people. They often become great "havers," but seldom great givers of themselves. Yet the secret of a happy life and even of a long secure job is learning to GIVE of yourself and your resources.

How our job makes us feel and what it helps us become as people is as important, if not more important, than what we gain from it by way of money and position. Few of us stop to measure the nonmonetary merits of our job.

I was really impressed with a sharp young woman who chatted with me once after one of my cleaning seminars. We were discussing what was a good job, and she said: "I worked in the snack bar of a bus depot once. It was a tough, marginal job and while I got only a few small tips, I found lots of people hungry for a little friendliness and caring. I left at night feeling rewarded and happy. Later I worked at one of the city's finest restaurants. I got big tips, but I was often serving ill-mannered people who showed no concern or respect for me. Looking back on my life now, that first job was the best I ever had."

Who we get to work with and around is also as important as position and money in the bank. A year or two working with the finest violinist or craftsperson in the world will pay us a hundred times the dividends over the next fifty years of our life, as starting at a big salary with guaranteed raises.

Before you ask for more money

Nearly all of us have found (often all too quickly) that no matter what we make, it isn't enough to buy all we want. Or to pay for all we've bought. So what the boss doesn't pay, we borrow, and most of us, even in our early teens, find ourselves owing more than we can earn. We seldom blame ourselves for this situation. First it's the recession, then the politicians, then those who earn interest on our indebtedness. But strangely, somehow it always ends up the fault of our job. Even if we agreed to our present wage or rate, if our ends don't meet we'll believe it's because the boss should pay more. When we find ourselves overbought and overplayed, we interpret this as overworked and underpaid. And we often get together with others who feel the same way and organize our new demands in the form of a strike.

A supplier for my business, for example, ran a nice company with several hundred employees. He was a good boss and he paid well and they all were happy. Then in the 70's many of them bought extra cars and bigger and better homes, and went on trips, etc., and found themselves in tight times. Ripe for

union promises now, they organized themselves under a pro negotiator and forcefully demanded a raise. Disappointed, the old owner shook his head slowly and said, "Okay, if that will make them happy, okay." The elated negotiator informed the workers that if the old man had caved in that easily on the first round, it was smart to demand even more. So next thing you know the committee filed into the owner's office with a new, bigger demand. The old boss shook his head slowly, got up, turned off the electricity at the main switch right in the middle of the day, then ordered everyone out of the building and locked it. They never put another bristle in another brush after that—they were all out of a job. "You can't do this," they and their lawyers yelled. "What will we do?" "I can and I did," the boss said, and he left the next morning for Europe for good. Bosses have limits and budgets, too.

Another time, a large, well respected national business announced that they were moving to our town. The local merchants were thrilled, as were the local unemployed, and headlines announced: "500 new jobs for the area." They paid much better than any existing employer, too. So they came and built and operated, and after two years all the employees demanded a bigger break room and longer breaks, covered parking, child care, a better health plan, more sick leave, and raises and more raises. The company yielded and yielded and then one day the headlines now announced: "Company to Leave City." A shocked and horrified mob of workers immediately demanded an explanation and the boss made it simple: "We can sell a pound of product competitively for $3.00. With the increased costs of production (two-thirds of them due to your demands), we'd have to sell it for $3.20. So we can't keep making it." And they did indeed leave.

In hundreds of cases like these we blame the company, failing to realize that the workplace has the same economics as the home place. When it costs more to live than you make, you can't live, and when it costs more to operate than you make, you can't operate. Then your job along with the boss's business is gone.

How soon can you expect a raise?

"Raise" (next to "time off") is the most magic word in the whole world of work. It's always there, that unspoken promise that someday you may have more and better, that suddenly the sun will burst out and warm your little wallet or purse... and it's all in the hands of your boss.

Well, not quite. The timing might be, but the *reasons* for a raise are 100% in *your* hands. You earn your own raises. Waiting for a raise or letting time or tenure or unions be your negotiator is wasting your time, emotion, and resources. Bosses love to give the deserving raises. It's their favorite thing to do because every raise you get, if earned and justified, means a raise in *their* position and profits. I'd love to double my people's salary and have and will again when they earn it by outstanding performance. That means more and better work, not mere time on the job. Raises are easy to get. Just earn them and if you turn out to be a top producer and the boss doesn't deliver, there are smarter and more perceptive bosses around who will (after they steal you). You have nothing to lose but low pay.

Raises and promotions: don't force the issue

Today there are hundreds of rules and laws to force bosses to be responsible and treat you well in the workplace, and there are thousands of attorneys dying to help you enforce any that might have been overlooked. Let me give you some good advice, though: Don't use legal channels to harass your boss or company or to attempt to force them to do something. You may score some quick points but you're going to lose the game. Likewise, don't let unions pressure anyone or try to speak for you. Do it yourself—you'll get further and feel better about it. I know sometimes legal means are all you can use and the only thing that will work. In cases like these I'd say go for it, the boss probably deserves it. But I'd use this only as a last resort to get action.

Kindness, understanding, patience, and accelerated output have secured more jobs and gotten more rights, privileges, and raises than all the union force in the last two centuries.

When you do anything to force a boss to respond to your wishes, you're clearly trying to take away his authority and right to run his business. Trust me, that never goes over well with any boss. You have little or no knowledge of all the reasons he does or doesn't do things, and to demand or pressure him in your direction is out-and-out rebellion. Force feeding never worked with any of us in babyhood, and you can be sure it doesn't in bosshood!

A boss should **want** to promote you and give you raises, not have to because of sex, race, creed, color, tenure, unions, or anything else you might use to jockey yourself into a better position on the job. I've always made it a policy to approach the deserving before they ask. I think it's a shame for anyone who's really performing to have to crawl to the boss and ask for a raise.

Forcing raises, promotions, and positions always ends up a bad situation for all concerned. "Have to" is a cut and dried branch, "want to" is a live and growing one.

Here are the things that will get you what you want, when you want it:

- **Performance**: Be the best and always be willing and always be there when the boss needs you.
- **Volunteering**: Initiative is the #1 spark to light any boss's fire.
- **Working well with your subordinates**: When you are seen working well together with your coworkers, it tells the boss that you're capable of having people work for you.
- **Helping the boss** (and his or her family, if they work there, too) reach their goals.
- **Being thankful for, and showing appreciation for, your job**: Don't just say so, show it.
- **Accepting your own life as your responsibility**: Don't blame your job or your boss for all your problems.

The importance of showing up

I met once with the retiring personnel manager of a large Florida hospital. In her 40 years on the job she hired and handled thousands and thousands of people ranging from priests to practical nurses, cleaners to computer operators. When I asked her what in her experience was the #1 cause of job loss (firings), she said it was, without question, "absenteeism." Ragged attendance is what runs most people off their jobs.

If you really want to be secure, want to be kept around in your job, want to get raises and promotions, the smartest move you can make is to be there, every single day you're supposed to be. A few years ago, there was a flood in New Orleans, and the world stopped to read the disaster story. Everything was cut off—traffic, electricity, phones, etc. and the whole city ground to a halt... except for one faithful janitor who had never missed a day of

work. He walked, waded, and swam 15 miles through cottonmouth-infested water, and he made it to the building he was entrusted with the care of... on time!

"Absence makes the heart grow fonder" may be true, but it usually means fonder of someone else. That's the way it is most of the time, especially in a job situation. When you aren't there, people do honor your excuses and adjust, but the wheels of alternatives or replacements are already turning. You can miss work and your calls can be routed, your territory temporarily handled by someone else, and your meetings rescheduled. But being gone is always negative, even when you're entitled to be gone.

I know people who haven't missed work in more than 30 years, and they're the real heroes in my book. Those who are always cutting time off the front and back and middle of their shift are slowly cutting themselves out of a job. So:

1. **Be there...** even if it's tough at times.

2. In an emergency, **worry about your replacement**, even if it's technically your supervisor's worry. Help and search and suggest and do whatever you can to make sure your area is covered, your work done, and your customers taken care of properly.

Some of us punch a clock, but most of us are on the honour system when it comes to our comings and goings, breaks and lunchtimes. A word to the wise here is: Give more than you take. On time is good, early is great! Did you ever stop to think that there's usually only about 5-8 minutes of difference between the person who leaves work first, and the one who leaves last? Think of the respect the boss has for that "last" leaver.

3. **Be on time...** no... *be a little early.* Early gives your bosses and fellow workers confidence in you, and it shows leadership potential. Early is ambitious, early feels good, and early covers some of your unintended slippage, too.

4. **Give a little extra**... beating the quitting whistle by 5 minutes beats you out of a lot of subtle advantages. Start giving 5 minutes every day instead of taking it and watch how much better things turn out for you.

Will all this go unnoticed? *Never!* Lots of times we think our faithful attendance and extra time and effort goes unnoticed by the big boss. Don't be fooled. Most big bosses got where they are through rigid attention to attendance and plenty of extra hours, so they do notice and will eventually reward you.

Do bosses weigh employees' sins?

Do they ever! We all have our little tolerances and indulgences with everyone we know and love and work with or for. You can often accept a few "F's" from an employee if they have a lot of T's (talents). Imperfection shows itself in the workplace more than anywhere else, and often talent can compensate for some real drawbacks, and enthusiasm can even compensate for lack of talent!

Some employees are unquestionably lazy, yet they do a lot for the company because they're so creative and smart. Some are just average in ability, yet they're worth top wage because they work twice as hard as anyone in the company. You always want to work to correct your weaknesses, for sure, but if you have strengths, strengthen them. Do anything you can to make the most of your computer wizardry or fleet feet and you'll be a star, even if you are a little shabby in one or two other areas.

Boy! Am I glad to be here!

The phone rang, my publicist Tobi took the call, and then hung up the phone. She grabbed the huge stack of mail that had just been dropped in front of her, quivered excitedly, and said "Oh, wow, I just can't wait for this day to happen!" She was really into her work and it showed. I happened to be walking by at the moment and it was music to my ears.

Another time I handed a worker a paycheck and she said, "Oh, Boy, all this action and excitement and I get paid for it, too! What a deal!"

Bosses love people who love their work. It's never a bad idea to show appreciation for the chance our job gives us to earn and learn and exercise our talents. Think how irritated you are when you hire a plumber, a mechanic, or someone to mow your lawn, and they show up grumbling about having to come at all, and are more intent on how much they're going to make, than on the job at hand.

Just a couple of years ago the Eureka Company hired me to demonstrate vacuums at a housewares show. It was a huge convention in a major city, with nine and a half miles of booths! They also hired a sleek professional model to assist, to hand out literature, direct traffic, and help out in general at the booth. She was well educated, personable, and unquestionably attractive, but unemployed most of the time, she told me. I found out why in the first fifteen minutes on the job. Here she had this great job for a super company, in an exciting place where she had a chance to meet and get to know a lot of important people. But it bored her.

I felt like a little kid at the fair. I was there an hour early, she arrived one minute to zero hour (the minimum time her contract called for). A Eureka executive led us both to the front of the display and explained what he wanted us to do. Before he could finish she interrupted to ask "When are my break times?" "Are you paying for lunch?" "How long is lunch hour?" And she sipped on a coffee the whole time the gentleman was instructing us. He was truly irritated—her beauty didn't compensate for her ingratitude. She acted as

if the entire $80,000 booth and every one of the company executives there all existed only for her convenience. As the day wore on she was a series of mechanical smiles to customers, in between glancing 400 times at her watch and sighing. She was amazed that in nine straight hours, I never left my post in the booth once, either to eat or use the bathroom. Customers from all over the world were constantly there and I didn't want to take a chance of missing one. She thought I was crazy, but I wasn't. I was grateful for the work. She was 500 times better looking than me, but they never hired her again. I was soon the Eureka spokesperson for the whole country. She might have been!

That eager attitude of truly appreciating your job doesn't just impress the boss. Believe it or not, it makes the work more enjoyable!

Should you do more than "your share"?

Sometime, somewhere in your life, you've got to decide whether you're going to be a real giver and doer, or one of the average hum-drummers just floating the stream of the job. People really worry about doing more than "their share." What is your share?

1. As much as others are doing?
2. More than others are doing?
3. Just what the boss is asking you to do?
4. What you are capable of?

Where did this "share" business come from? What kind of person do you want to be? One that sets goals, and lives by comparison? Or one that sets goals, and lives by capacity? There's merit in doing what's expected on the job, sure, but it's no fun and no way to

establish your life pattern either. Who wants a rubber stamp rating—"better" is so much better. Better than expected is beautiful, always working harder and smarter, regardless of the pay or the day. Every real winner I've known is someone who always gives 150%, even on a minimum wage job or a volunteer unpaid job. A good person will work and strive as hard for free as for $10,000 a month.

On the other hand, I've seen thousands of employees adjust their effort to the pay rate. This is really dumb, because once you find the "get-by gear" and run very long in it, it becomes your only gear. This sure limits your ability to get ahead.

I had a salaried employee once who got offended over some little injustice and went on a two-week "I'll show you" trip and gave, to the second, what was required, nothing more. He did his job, coming through the door stiff-necked at exactly 8:00 a.m., looking only straight ahead like a robot, speaking only as strictly necessary to do the job. He was determined not to give a mite more or less than he was being paid for. He was half as productive as before, miserable the whole time, and everyone was snickering at him for it. It was a perfect classic tantrum (learned at the age of three). And he ended up the loser. One of those little extra territory-expanding assignments came up during that time, and because of his unwillingness for any early, late, or extra, it was permanently passed to someone else (who kept and enlarged upon it and got a raise and praise). Minimum effort minimizes you!

Few of us think about our effect on our fellow workers. Many of them are new, discouraged or demoralized, having problems at home, etc. Our own attitude can help or hurt them immensely. I've seen lots of good ambitious new people come to a bad end because the people they came in contact with on the job were lazy, or whiners and bitchers and complainers. Your co-workers will always look up to and follow you, so you have a real chance to make a difference here.

Taking the Initiative...

Is the sweetest music ever played on a boss's heartstrings. In other words doing what's needed and right without having to be told (or begged or served notice), volunteering to help take up the slack when someone obviously needs to, even taking some work home occasionally. This is initiative, and bosses love it.

Doing what you're expected to is doing your job; doing more than expected or assigned is promotable behavior.

One good way to take the initiative is to have and make use of a spare time list. Everyone gets lulls or "waiting time," and too many of us think this is nothing but a breather. If you have to wait around for half the morning while they locate a new part for your word processor, the boss is still paying you for that time, and you should still be working, even if something isn't lined up and you aren't commanded to do it. So just make a list, or even ask, what you might do if you get some extra time (see p. 58).

Peacemakers get promoted

I still remember Mother's formula for a happy home: "With all the problems, hate, and war in the world, at least here at home we can have peace and love." And we did, and it was wonderful.

The workplace can and should be the same—there's no sense or benefit in having friction or negativism at work. As bosses know only too well, even a tiny disagreement unresolved can really affect productivity.

Disagreements, vendettas, petty jealousies, skirmishes, snide remarks, and other attacks

around the job are **war**—plain and simple. Just as shooting wars kill, injure, and impoverish a country, so do "work wars" kill and injure incentive, teamwork, progress, and enthusiasm. The time and money wasted in all this also affects the bottom line of the balance sheet. And that bottom line is important not just to the boss, but to all of us. All of our pay, perks, benefits, and employment security comes from that bottom line. You better be a good soldier and strengthen it, not tear it down.

No matter how good a worker you may be, if you're a troublemaker, you are your boss's enemy. At work, as anywhere, you can find a fight in every situation if you hunt hard enough. Rabble rousing may help you and others blow off steam, but it won't get you anywhere in the long run, because one of those people you don't get along with will harpoon you. Remember, an enemy today may be your boss tomorrow. So **everyone** should be in your peace plan.

The ability to get along with everyone will make you a real number one with your boss. If you're a peacemaker among your colleagues, you'll win praises and raises. Bosses know how much trouble costs.

But what about politics? Won't they help me get ahead?

No. Politics are a pitiful way to piddle away your life, on or off the job. What do I mean by politics?

Plotting, scheming, jockeying, wedging, busybodying, building little walls, digging little holes, laying traps, dodging traps, faking, playing dumb, setting people up for things, bluffing, paying people off, pulling strings, passing the buck, lying, exaggerating, engineering, kissing butts, laughing at unfunny jokes, undermining friends and foes, attending things you hate, saying things you don't believe, stonewalling, planting seeds, sucking up to, getting chummy with, sleeping with, flirting with, favor doing, gift buying, cocktail party inviting, hint dropping, eavesdropping, bugging/tapping, opening others' mail, going through the wastebaskets, territory invading, account snatching, gratuity giving, under the tabling, off the recording, fiddling with the books, leveraging, shifting, circumventing, wrangling, angling...

...all to get some little gain or false advantage.

What a waste of good work time and energy. Politics will take all too much of your wit, effort, and wisdom at work or anywhere. "But everyone does it." Maybe so, but if you don't you'll be ahead of everyone else and out of trouble.

Having words with your boss

Of the hundreds of thousands of words that could be exchanged between you and the boss, two little expressions are truly magic, when used in either direction—from the boss to you or from you to the boss:

Thank you

I'm sorry

One day I was complaining to my wife that although I'd done at least twenty great, gracious, overgenerous things for my employees over the past year, almost none of them had said thank you. One fall, for example, I set a little goal (which I knew they could easily reach) and said that if they did so, I'd give each of them a $1000 check on Thanksgiving Day. There were seven people involved here, and some of them made less than that in a month. I did it halfway as a gift and I felt good about it. Only one of the seven came to me and thanked me.

As I was moaning and groaning about this, my wife asked me when was the last time I said thank you to them? I thought about it, and it was true that my lips hadn't formed those words any more often than theirs had. I might have mumbled a "Mahalo" (which is thanks in Hawaiian), but they didn't know, so I was guiltier than they.

Bosses are human, too. I know you inwardly feel the boss *owes* you an extra nicety or two from time for all that hard work you've done for them over the months and years. But when they do come through for you, let them know that you appreciate it, don't just think it. We all like to hear the words.

Good housekeeping is job keeping

If you want to gain some real ground with the boss, keep your grounds (workspace) neat and clean. Even bosses who are out-and-out slobs themselves really appreciate this. It's the squared-away who usually get promoted. Even if you're barely able to wade through the dirt and clutter to cross the room at home, and couldn't possibly find the floor of your car, don't bring that same housekeeping approach to work with you. It will really hurt your chances of keeping and enjoying your job. It's a clear signal to the boss that you don't care, that you'll accept any standard or level. It's also a big safety risk.

Now one last big one:

Make sure you understand the objectives and instructions your boss has given you

"It's better to ask dumb questions than to make stupid mistakes" sums up this all-important phase of doing your job well and keeping the boss appreciating you. We joke about this all too common and serious problem: "Well, as soon as I figure out what my job is, I'll tell you." I've seen officefuls of employees asked to write out their job descriptions, and only a few of them could. They kind of all just show up and work behind the leader. Many had no idea of what they were doing or why, or how long it should take.

Quit trying to manage the boss and start managing yourself, and you'll get all you're after.

You've probably heard, too, about the man who walked by a construction site and asked the first fellow he saw what he was doing. "Laying bricks," was the answer. He asked the next worker, too, and he said "Laying bricks." And so on with three more, always the same answer. The sixth person he asked said: "We're building a new school for the community." He was the only one who really knew what they were doing. "Laying bricks" was the work, but the job was building a school.

This is often a bigger error on the boss's part than the employees'. Many bosses never really make clear what they want, how long it should take, or when they want it done. They just turn you loose. I've certainly been guilty of this. In my mind I know the goal and the vision, I see the end result. Then I assign everyone a piece of the work and too often forget to tell them what we're working toward and why.

If your boss doesn't tell you all you need to know to feel really good about what you're doing, then ask him or her. It's for your benefit. If you don't, you'll be like the old folks losing their hearing who don't know what was said but refuse to ask. You may be too proud, or you just don't want to admit you don't know or didn't hear. Don't be that way. Ask and keep asking.

Work is a lot more fun when you know exactly what you're doing and why. It's a lot easier to put your shoulder to the wheel when you know where the wagon is headed.

Chapter 6

When Your Job Starts Getting to You

Nothing describes the feelings we sometimes have toward our jobs better than this note, which one of my managers found on his desk along with a set of building keys:

Mr. Stoker,
I have decided to quit my job. I just can't take it anymore.
Sorry.
Ellis
Didn't have the heart to tell you in person!

Ellis was working 14-hour days, in the toughest, grimiest, most inappreciative section of the complex we were contracted to clean. He had the worst hours, too. When I saw the note I didn't blame him, in fact it warmed my heart with compassion.

We've all composed similar messages at least mentally when our job begins to match our discouraged mood, and like Ellis, we may have reached the point where it really is time to move on or out. However, any job has its ups and downs, and before you leave let me tell you about all the other "Ellises" who at certain times were on the verge of getting out, quitting, but didn't. And later they were glad they didn't, because they went on to enjoy some great rewards from their jobs. I'll bet thousands of people a day lose or leave good jobs because they were getting a little battle weary and the last straw was a bad problem that came along on a day when they happened to come to work in no mood. I've found that the majority of people who quit do it hastily and often for some minor cause, and then regret it later. I don't know of a job, even among million-dollar-a-year ball players, movie stars, ski instructors, doctors, lawyers, and airline pilots, where they don't sometimes reach a "fed up" point and want to walk away. The dissatisfaction often isn't with the job at all, it's with ourselves or some other personal frustration or circumstance in our lives. So don't be too quick to blame your job and quit it because "It's getting you down."

When one of those sour moments in your life or job comes along (and they always will), I'd sure hate to see you yield to some momentary emotion and put yourself out of a job, when you might have found other, much less expensive and upsetting alternatives. You aren't the first and won't be the last to suffer from the job blahs or blues. Over the years I've collected some pretty good first aid solutions for this from my own experience and that of many others who have faced and gone through it. The following are the big ones.

Quitting is rarely the answer

I have a coaching degree, and I lettered in both high school and college athletics. Participating in sports is much like holding down a job—both help build our character, and both have bosses. A good athletic coach, like a good boss in business, can be a real inspiration, just so-so, or pure hell to work or play under. And unfortunately, we all sooner or later do encounter the boss or coach we just don't like. They may even be totally intolerable, and something or someone has to give. You can be pretty sure it isn't going to be the person in the power position, the coach or boss.

In more than thirty-five years of bossing at least 40,000 people and coaching at least as many—high school, Scouts, Little League, and church teams—I've learned there's a critical point here: that time when things cave in, people quit, and lives are rerouted, some scars can be created here that never heal. A few months ago, for example, I patted the head of a fine talented boy and asked him how ball playing was going this summer. "He isn't playing, he didn't join this year," his mother volunteered. I was shocked, the kid loved ball and was in Little League prime. "Why?" I asked. "He had his differences with the coach and he doesn't like him," she said. I've heard this same exact thing from others any number of times, so I asked the pair the question you should ask yourself in such circumstances, at work or play. "Whether you like or dislike

them, are you going to let a single person, a coach [or boss] keep you out of a sport [or job] you like and need? This could affect the whole rest of your life!" They'd never thought about that, only that they were "showing" the coach. So the team played on while the boy sat in front of the TV and ate Oreos, growing butt instead of muscle.

There's a sort of whiney myth around that if you don't like something and it happens to be uncomfortable or stressful, if the person in charge is too tough or demanding, you can just quit (the team, club, job) and your problems are over. Maybe so—but you really haven't accomplished anything, because the next team or job, or the one after that, could make some equally mean demands on you, or maybe worse. Far better to learn how to cope with anything that comes along.

Nobody is tougher than a marine drill sergeant. He is worse than tough, he is mean and without question he is the boss, and all the new momma's boys he gets on his team don't like him much. In fact most of them hate his guts, but they're afraid to kill him, so they just want to quit like they did back on the team, in school, or on the job. But they don't quit, they stick it out—learn, train, and obey, and say "Sir, sir, sir, sir..." until their lip automatically curls into an "S." Then something strange happens, they not only survive the game of training, they're proud of it. They actually like and respect that sergeant now... and they like themselves much better, too.

Too many people find out, after a job and a boss is gone, that they actually had a pretty good job and a pretty good boss.

Every job, every game, every marriage, every everything has its moments of opposition—more than just moments—more like weeks and months, even years. If you end up in a nasty, almost intolerable work situation, it might be the boss and it might be you, and you might need to go all the way and make a change. I'd just like to caution you that sometimes enduring and blooming where you are planted is the best route to take to building a good life and job security. Almost everyone who has a super job situation (and goes on to their 25th year, with the same company or boss) will tell you that they, like the young man with the coach, had tense times somewhere along the line. But they didn't walk away. No matter whose fault it was. They stuck it out, figured it out, and then worked it out, every one of them did. Many of us have had loser teachers, loser coaches, or even loser parents, but they can only foul up your life if you let them. So this is my first advice: When things start to cave in on the job, don't think quit or run, or start the cold shoulder routine.

There is almost a 100% chance that you'll have times of trouble and anxiety on your job, that you'll come up against unfairness, ingratitude, even being assigned to work with a bunch of jerks on a crew. Just remember that *you* basically control the situation, the amount and quality of work that you do. The situation doesn't control you. So keeping your mouth shut, doing a good job, and working your way through it all is your first and best option.

On the other hand, if a boss is so awful, dishonest, incompetent, or horny that you have to violate your own character and conscience to be associated with him, then leaving is a good thing to do. No job is worth degrading yourself for.

Don't quit just to get attention

Sometimes a boss isn't mean or bad and may even pay you well, but he or she takes you completely for granted. This can be as bad as a beating and even worse than firing. It's sad, but bosses and companies can get insensitive to even exceptional people. They can get so that even 180% effort is just expected and they seldom thank the person for it or even notice it. If this happens to you, then do something clever to get recognition.

Clever doesn't have to mean crooked or crafty, because there is even a scripture that says, "Let thy good work be known." The thing to be careful about here is making sure you really *are:* (A) Outstanding, and (B) Unappreciated. If you just "think" you are, and go to great ends to reveal your work more explicitly to the boss (and it turns out to not be all that great), it could backfire.

Whenever superiors aren't patting you on the head and singing the hymns of praise in your honor that you feel you deserve:

1. Drop them a nice "thank you for the job" letter and end it listing as humbly as possible your endless contributions to the cause (and their profits).

2. When you visit with them (in some get-together that *they've* initiated), find a way to work in the same nonobnoxious summary of your love of the job and of all the efforts you're putting out and what **more** you could do? (This really makes them look and listen.)

3. Find a mediator (someone who is really impressed with, and respects you), and work out a way for them to do some "second-hand" or proxy bragging about you to the boss. (It should all be honest and objective, of course.)

4. Leave for a while! (for any "legal" or constructive reason—marry, go on a mission or a long vacation, take a leave of absence to write your memoirs, etc.). Yes, this is risky, but real doers make more brownie points by being gone than you can imagine. The gaping hole you leave, that takes the boss two temporaries and an extra shift to fill, will get unforgettable attention. It works every time. However if you happen not to be the rising star you imagine you are, and they can do your job without adding anyone, you're in big trouble!

Quitting, or leaving for good, of course, really gets attention. But it always pushes someone's "pride" button, and even if you and the boss are bleeding to get back together, usually one or both of you just won't yield and all is lost.

To get right down to the bottom line, even when a job appears to be caving in, the situation is still largely in your court.

A bad boss can't hold you back

Remember that even the worst boss or company can't hold back a really good employee—think on that a minute. Some of you will run into a boss, for example, who when you do well, and then better and better, starts worrying that you are going to outshine him. So he will try to cut you down or cut you back, give you garbage assignments, anything to get rid of you. We both know what you can do about that. You can do the garbage assignment so well the boss will bawl. You can shine even if they throw tar on you. And what a great way to get even with a bad boss. As the scriptures tell us: turn the other cheek and heap coals of fire on their heads. It works like magic.

"Middle man" bosses

We do encounter bosses that seem to have been made boss because the company couldn't figure out what else to do with them. They're really failures, kind of middle man bosses, often bossed badly themselves, and given one or two people of their own to boss (like we give an ornery tiger a piece of meat to chew on and work out their aggression).

If you get stuck with one of these, you'll seldom change them, so either suffer or change jobs. Bad deals do come along. My cleaning company had one in Phoenix, a fellow who before every meeting would announce, "I'm paid to be a mean butt and I'm going to be one, too." We did everything, even crawl, and he only got worse. He was a disgrace to bosshood, so if you think every boss is going to be perfect just because he or she is a boss, guess again! I tell you this so you won't be surprised and want to give up. Situations like this will give you great practice and experience in making even bad decisions work. And you'll learn what you don't want to be like when you are a boss.

When you suddenly find yourself working for someone who was once your equal

A toughie, and it often reminds me of an aunt of mine who planned and planned and planned an outdoor event. She sewed dresses and tablecloths for it, ordered centerpieces for it, made exotic salads and desserts and other dishes to serve, cleaned up the whole yard and even bought a new picnic table and put in a new patio for the occasion. It was indeed going to be a masterful celebration and display for the club members she invited. It was scheduled for August, when the chances of rain in Idaho are about one half of one percent, but rain it did. It poured buckets, and all was lost or ruined. I can still remember her out there looking up at the sky in tears, saying "This can't be happening to me." But it was, and someday, maybe even more than one someday, a cloud burst will pour into your life in the form of a former equal (or even subordinate) who is promoted over you. Now she is your boss, and it doesn't mean she is superior, only that she is your boss. You report to her and take orders from her, and you may find this as intolerable or unfair as the rain that ruined my aunt's entire year. But it happens. In fact you might even be the boss in question here, promoted over more worthy peers. Too many times we let these unjust or surprise promotions wash us up. If you're going to be somebody in life you have to learn to handle rainy days. Commit yourself to making the sun shine on the new deal no matter how many clouds have gathered around, and watch. You'll become the king or queen of the ball before long. Injustice only injures you if you allow yourself to sink in it. Make any boss look good, and you'll look better!

Doubled teamed

Boy, is this a common one, and does it put us in a bind. How often in our work lives will it happen:

Your boss tells you to do something and how to do it and you go for it. Then along comes the big boss, the owner, the king, your boss's boss, who looks at the work a lot more like you do. And he tells you a new way, the way he wants it done. Suddenly you're in a crossfire—you've been doing it well as you were told and now who do you follow? If you quickly change course to please the big kahuna, then your boss (the one you have to work with every day) is going to be bent out of shape. Little bosses hate this sort of thing, too. After they've been given position and authority, to have someone interfere with or override them! This happens a million times a day. It's one of those management quirks that will never go away as long as humans run things.

Here you have only one intelligent move: quickly state the assignment and instructions of your immediate boss. "This is how I was told to do it—would you like me to do it differently? This often brings the enthusiastic interferer to their senses and they'll go to your boss and discuss it (like they should have to begin with). If they insist on jumping over your boss, be sure to inform your direct boss of your bind, and make sure he knows you told his boss of your loyalty to him. (Sounds like a soap opera.)

Don't play both ends to the middle, it's trouble no matter what you do. Just do your best to minimize conflict. Confusing as it might be sometimes, the ultimate power is higher up. They own the place, they hired your boss, and they do have the right to override. So don't let this get to you and don't ever, ever fuel any fire between the bosses—you'll be the one that burns!

Don't let someone else force you to leave

What do you do when someone on the job (at any level) is making you miserable? Lots of us finally grew out of being teased and tormented by our big brothers or sisters or the school bully, only to find out now, at work, that there are people (our clients, customers, or peers) who live only to embarrass or irritate us. These ornery sorts exist in every business and can cause real job unhappiness, with their continual pettiness and picking on us. Whether a saint or a sinner we all have something—traits, habits, successes, looks, pay, or position—that bugs certain people, and they'll slip the dagger to us every chance they get. I've had clients who didn't even know me personally, for example, who constantly and expertly undermined my job for no other reason than that they wanted their kids to be doing the cleaning and make the money for doing it. In janitorial work, clients will purposely leave their place an incredible mess, or hide or sabotage your supplies and equipment, or start rumors and gossip about you. And some will just hide out and shift all the work onto you, not do their share and you get the blame.

I don't need to tell you that any job is tough enough without some idiot working overtime to aggravate you. Mother always told us to just ignore teasing and picking and the teaser would soon quit, although slugging or some other less subtle form of revenge always seemed more appropriate for such nitwits. Tattling, whimpering, and whining to Mother never got us anywhere and only delighted our tormentor. Nor will it help here. Only when we fight a tormentor or try to retaliate do they feel fully successful. The number one solution is to go on the offensive in a different way, kill them with kindness and service. It'll make them look dumb if not obnoxious. Create an atmosphere of giving to them so generously that their own guilt will blot out their problems and you'll win a friend, not just stop the aggression. I'd find out what's really bugging them, if you can. Maybe it's just your cologne or shaving lotion. You don't have to do this in a head-to-head confrontational way: "Okay, jerk, what's your problem?" Just do a little gentle investigation to find out why they're after you. Once you discover what it is, you can often avoid or eliminate it.

People who are out to irritate others generally have low self-esteem, and they want and need attention. When you transform someone like that into one of your champions, it's a real accomplishment.

Is someone invading "your territory"?

Here, in one of the most basic (and maybe basest) of human instincts—territory—we're just like the animals. We get uptight about it. Once we stake our claim to any area of responsibility, we mark it well and we own it, at least we think we do. It's ours, mentally, physically, and emotionally, it's written right there on our job description below our name. And then... some stranger, new person or outlaw approaches, and encroaches. They start doing the editing or sweeping or answering the phones or unlcading, some job we'd always done, a job we carved out of the wilderness of the waiting room, pioneered and developed and nurtured. Now someone else has it or is taking it (and all its glory) away! Even if it's for the better somehow, doesn't this just kill us?

Taking someone else's assignments seems to amount to the worst of all insults. But progress often demands changes and shifts of assignments, and bosses have the ugly job of saying when and how and where and who. Seldom does the result please everyone, even if they're convinced it's for the good. They're still irritated and go home and complain to the family about it after they're finished complaining to everyone at work about it.

We need to remember something about work here: All assignments or positions are just functions or parts of a bigger job the boss and the whole company are working together to get done.

No matter how crushed you are, don't whine and whimper and limp around with a hangdog look for the next two years. No matter how disappointing and unfair it seems, jump in and bend your back and yes, help the "claim jumper" find the gold. I promise if you do, you get more gold than you ever mined while you had the claim.

What if the boss asks you to do something that isn't right?

It can happen and does happen hundreds of times every day. You are asked to sign, say, sell, or present something that both you and the boss know is wrong, questionable, shady, even crooked. What do you do? If you don't do what you've been asked, you get fired. And you wouldn't really be the guilty one, would you? You'd just be doing your job, doing as you're told. *Wrong*—even that first little seed of action will blossom into a big problem for you. If you did it, just because you were told, try convincing a jury of that after you're indicted for it. If you knew it was wrong and you did it anyway, you're dead. I'd let them fire me first.

Employee evaluations

You ought to know pretty well where you stand before going in for that one-on-one visit with your boss in the middle or at the end of the year. You've actually prepared for it a whole year or six months ahead, by your actions on the job every day.

If you don't know, or have any idea and don't like what it is, you'll probably be nervous. And whether you've committed grave errors or done great good, forty-five minutes before is a poor time to plan strategy. The right way to handle an evaluation is to write a up a list, well before the meeting, of questions or issues you'd like to discuss. Then when you go into the evaluation, never talk about yours first, just listen and cross off the ones the boss has already beat you to as he goes through his list. When he or she is finished with their points, bring up yours. And whether what you hear is good or bad, you always want to respond, not react. If it's a negative, back off and be humble and find out why. If it's a positive, be sure to say thanks and reaffirm your commitment to better performance next year.

Evaluations are prepared for a long time in advance, so be sure to do your side months ahead, too.

Find out where you stand if you need to

If you are in what you feel may be a difficult or questionable situation with your boss or your company, or if you don't even know where you are or where you stand, it can really be nerve-wracking. There's a smart and easy thing you can do about it—*ask*.

I find it interesting that even after I know someone for a while and they are telling me about their job, if I ask them "Is your boss happy with you?" it always catches them off guard. Seldom do I get a positive answer. What I hear is "Well, I don't know..." or "I think so..." or "Gosh, I hope so..." Gads, I'd say that knowing where you are on the road of your employment is more crucial than knowing where you are on the interstate. Ask! Your boss will welcome the chance to tell you either way. And either way, you need to know. If your boss isn't happy with you, find out, before the job or the relationship fizzles out.

How do you ask? Inoffensively. Find a private time and place, smile, and say. "Mrs. Spath, I love working here. How am I doing?" Most bosses are a little soft and chicken-hearted down deep, and will often give you the automatic answer, "Fine, Walter, just fine." That hasn't told you anything. So here's how you find out. Your next question is the one that hits pay dirt (no pun intended): "Is there anything you'd like me to do better?" Now watch and listen, and you'll find out how you're doing!

Remember what they said, write it down right away, and thank them. Then DO IT!!! If you do, they'll never forget it. Even if they were about to fire you that night, they'll change their mind and help you now. Because *you* were the initiator of the improvement, and made it easier for them.

Wanting to know where you stand from time to time is one thing, *but*

Job paranoia

Is something else again. It's one of the worst employment diseases going. The minute you get a job, you begin worrying if it's going to end—if the company is going to go down, someone is going to ace you out, or the boss is going to fire you. One of the best and most productive employees I ever had, one I praised constantly and bragged up to everyone I saw, had a habit of asking me to fire her. Anytime she did any little thing that might be questionable, she'd say, "Well, you ought to fire me for that." If she was gone a day or two for personal reasons or vacation, the first thing she'd say when she returned was: "Well, I see none of the locks are changed, I guess I'm still working here." It happened so often that just for the fun of it, I kept a little slip of paper in my top drawer, and every time she'd make some kind of "fire me" remark, like "Is my pink slip in here?" when I'd hand her any kind of envelope, I made a note of it. One month she asked me to fire her 22 times! (All the while I was thinking how much raise to give her.)

Lots of us get this way, sometimes with good cause, but good cause or not, never suggest your termination to your boss, even in jest. It's bad business. Most bosses won't even have thought of it until you bring it up, and once you do, you plant the seed of the possibility that maybe you *want* them to fire you.

Paranoia—thinking that everyone, from the boss to the clients to the janitor, is out to get you—is a poison in the workplace because:

1. Once you believe this sort of thing, you begin to live it and incorporate it into your job and attitude, and everything always comes out negative.
2. It's contagious. Before long even the open-minded innocents who never even gave a moment's thought to such things will be ducking and cringing and not knowing why.

Prepared is carrying an umbrella around on a rainy day. Paranoia is putting the umbrella up when there isn't a cloud in sight.

Stay clear of the shortcut sharpies

If you don't want to worry about having your job cave in on you, then stay out of the caves. One of the most dangerous underground tunnels around is hanging around and listening to the people at work who've found a way to beat the system. Those who know all the little shortcuts for getting more with less effort. Kids figure it out in the classroom and workers in the spud fields : "Hey Harry, if you grab the right side of the truck going up the rows and the left side going down, you'll get the light end of the sacks every time." Or, "Try to take your break at 10:30—that's when most of the work comes in—let the other suckers do it." Or "Come here, and I'll show you how to get two sandwiches out of the company cafeteria for the price of one."

You'll find these short circuit sharpies on any job, the easy-way worshippers who will clue you in on how to do the least possible for your pay. They can and will be your worst enemy. Avoid them!

Concentrate on making the wheels turn instead of wheeling and dealing. There are expert coasters in any work force—they're the easiest of all to spot, and the first ones the boss wants to get rid of. If you hang around with them, you'll look just like one of them and your job will be as vulnerable as theirs to termination.

Troublemakers, too, are among the first to go!

Since babyhood some of us have constantly brewed and used "trouble" to get attention: throwing tantrums, "wising off," or spreading gossip to keep ourselves the center of attention. This has no place in the workplace, where concentration on and dedication to the cause is our goal. Peacemakers always rise to the top in the long run, whereas bosses lay awake at night planning ways to get rid of the troublemakers. How do they recognize the troublemakers? Easy—it's those folks who seem to be there at every confrontation. This is bad business. You want to avoid troublemaking situations, avoid making any kind of public "scene," and avoid being one of the people involved. If you have a problem, work it out with the person or people involved, or work it out yourself, in private. Especially avoid dragging the boss in. Remember arbitration always means aggravation, and neither of you need that.

Avoid confrontations

Some of us have been known to get fed up with an assignment, some real or imagined ill treatment, or an obnoxious co-worker, to the point of being ready to blow someone's head off. So we finally do blow up, right in front of the boss—poor, poor policy. Stay away from the boss until you're calm and logical, and then softly, persuasively, state your case.

Bosses hate confrontations. When someone confronts me and informs me "It's either them or me," "me" will probably go first. Giving bosses ultimatums takes away their decision-making responsibility. You're taking it upon yourself to make a judgement for their business, and they don't like that. If you are planning to serve any notice or make any ultimatums, I'll advise you right now to prepare for the worst, because you're going to get it.

On going for the grass that's greener

It's only natural—no matter who we are or what job we have, every time a little dose of discomfort comes along, we find ourselves thinking of or looking for a "better job." Often this can preoccupy you to the point that you spend more time looking for a better job than you do doing your job, or trying to do your job better. Do that very long and you'll get a real chance at your dream of a different job!

As for those resumes everyone likes to "have ready," I was writing once, with the aid of their three top managers, a comprehensive houseservice administration manual for General Telephone in one of their California office complexes. This was going to save the company millions on their maintenance, was way overdue, and we were eight days into the project, approaching completion! The next morning it was announced that the entire Los Gatos GTE office would be closed down within a few months—and that place full of executives went on a rampage. Suddenly personal resumes put the whole place out of production and commission—they even took two floors of our word-processing people off the manual we were working on. Those of us with important companywide business to tend to were dead, so we all flew home, and it was months before the two days left on that project were finished.

This is just one of the reasons I'm kind of negative about resumes. They are like a health history made up without a doctor, valid only as history and publicity, not as any measure of your value or ability.

Lists of classes, degrees, and dates don't impress prospective bosses, they only care about productivity. Somebody's reference—"Damn, she's good"—will do you more good than an impeccably typeset form, on the best bond paper. They say little about production or performance, even if you've produced and performed. Not one of the 100 top producers I know has a resume, they don't need one. If it's stylish to have one, or you need one to graduate from How to Inflate a Resume 101, do them on your own time and copier!

A friend of mine, when the construction industry dipped, was laid off along with hundreds of others. He took his resume around to builders, they looked at it (it was good and so was the guy) and said, "Wow, you've built skyscrapers and engineered bridges—you're too rich for our blood, too high powered for our simple work." After being turned down again and again, he took his resume right out of the hands of the next boss and said: "Tell you what, I'm good, I guarantee it. Just give me a job, pay me what you're paying the lowest man on your crew, and I'll give you my best."

He was hired, and within two weeks the formerly unemployed man was boss of that job and many after.

Don't let a piece of paper speak for you, speak for yourself, with action and ability. Getting on the job is all you need if you're worth what you think you are.

If you do get a job offer from somewhere else

If you're worth even half your salt on this earth, you're going to run into lots of new and better opportunities while you are getting along well where you are. It happens in everything—life, love, and work. If you have a pulse, you should be interested in something better, and in growing, if the opportunity promises that. The problem is timing and ethics. Someone is treating and paying you well, has invested in and trained you and promised you a future, and now something else, much better for your future, comes up. You stumble on it or it's offered to you. Upgrading yourself is a right you have and one any good boss should honor. I'd ask myself just two questions if I were you:

Is this the right new opportunity for me?
When is the right time to leave/change?

Remember that when you're on a date you don't blab about how nice the one last night was (compared to the one you're on now). You might know it and think it, but you don't say it. I'd gather all the information you need about the other job, and do all the thinking and praying or whatever about the possibilities before I rocked the boat—buzzed my new possibilities around or told the boss about them.

When and if you do want to change, be up front about it. In almost every case I know of, when an employee, one I respect, comes to me about a better opportunity, it ends up a positive for both of us. If you're sneaky, on the other hand, and brag around and flash the offer to others before your boss, you probably won't have a choice of whether to go or not. Regardless of what you decide, you'll be gone.

A couple of other little extras here now that the schoolbooks don't teach you:

1. Never use an offer from elsewhere as a club to beat your current boss. "Hey, you're paying me $5.75 an hour and the guy down the street is offering me $6.25. What are you going to do about it?" Bad taste and bad tactics... never corner or chisel a boss or bargain with someone else's promises.

2. When and if you decide to change, double your output for the remaining time with the place you're now working. Never slack off, even if you're sure you'll never be there again. Leave the space clean and the work caught up when you leave and you will be rewarded many times over. Remember, you might get fired the first week of your next job and either have to go back to the old one or get a reference. Sure would be nice to be up for that either way.

Pay attention to Pecking Order

It started right in babyhood with big or little brother or sister. There was always an order to be observed and channels to go through, in all the years of growing up. The same was true in school, in the army or navy, in sports, or in your home town or city. There was a chain of command, a pecking order to be aware of, and any time you violated it, skipped the person in direct charge or responsibility and went directly to the top, you suffered for it. If the neighborhood bully was thrashing you and you went to the school authorities or the police, and they thrashed the bully, you could count on the bully nailing you twice as bad next time. On the job, even if your boss, the person you report to, is a real loser, if you go around them and go to your boss's boss with your needs and problems, your life around there will be all but over.

A truly desperate situation might merit skipping your direct boss with something, but be prepared for the wrath of the wounded, skipped boss. It will come.

On going to the rescue

The time will come when one of your best friends gets fired or ill treated on the job, and it seems that the only right and moral thing to do is come to their rescue with full unyielding support. This is an admirable way of thinking, but before you walk out on the limb of "If they go, I go," remember that you may not know all the circumstances of the case. How many times have you seen people you'd have sworn were faultless appear in the local or national news for robbery, rape, embezzlement, wife beating, drunk driving, or some other misdeed you'd never have imagined? It happens every day and it happens on the job. In my own company, for example, we've had highly respected, longtime employees do some rotten thing that merited not merely firing but jail. But after we let them go, a mob of their buddies would appear, knowing nothing about the situation, really, but ready to offer themselves as sacrifices to keep the guy's job. If you're 100% sure of a person's worthiness and innocence, you might want to support them to the death, but I'd be cautious here. Back off and find out all you can about the charges before you charge!

The new boss

You've got a good boss and you love her and all is going great. You even have her just about trained as to how good you are. Then (isn't it just your luck) suddenly the company moves her somewhere else and gives you another boss. You've had no say in choosing him, of course, he just appears one day and is introduced as "your new boss." Your immediate reaction, and that of most employees in this situation, is that this one couldn't

possibly be as good as the one you had. So (waiting for him to prove himself) you act cold and reserved and this causes the same response from the new boss, who instantly gets the signal that you don't like him or her.

When a new boss comes in, the key to making things work is actually *you*. After all, the boss is new to all this, but you've been around a while and know the lay of the land. You can make his job a lot easier, if you want to. Well I promise you that if you do, your help and kindness won't go unnoticed or unrewarded.

A great guru of a very large and successful business said to me once: "One of our ironclad rules is: Never do business with anyone you don't like." Overall I think that is a good one. Before I quit doing business with someone, however, I'd put some effort into finding out why I don't like them or they don't like me. And then see if I could amend it. Healed fractures are usually stronger than the original bone.

Remember that there are a lot of you and only one of him (the new boss). So you can learn and remember his name and needs much easier and faster then he can get all of yours. I'd be the aggressor, introduce yourself if you haven't been introduced, and welcome him. If you already know him, pledge your support in his new position and offer to help. Your status was probably passed on from the old boss to the new anyway, so you really only have one choice with a new boss, to make sure he or she succeeds.

Do give notice if you decide to go!

If you've really had enough and know you want to leave a job, fine. If you feel that strongly it's probably a good decision, and both you and the boss will benefit. Whatever you do, however, do give proper notice that you are leaving. Walking off the job, or waiting until you have something else lined up and then leaving with just one day's notice, will be a big mistake. Even if you want revenge on your boss, leaving without notice will eventually boomerang on you. If you come to me for a job and I find out (which I will) that you gave next to no notice on your last job and then just left, my immediate thought will be that you'll probably do the same to me... and I won't hire you. Even in the most negative parting, it's important to be professional and give two weeks notice or more if it's really needed in the type of job you happen to have. On the other hand, if you really need to leave quickly, ask if it might be possible. Often bosses will surprise you and let you go immediately if you ask, and in my company we often give a week's pay even to people we haven't been happy with.

Those who walk off the job... earn themselves an unmarketable reputation.

If you are fired or laid off

It happens... sometimes justly and sometimes unjustly. We lose our job or our position. Generally our first impulse is to look for someone to blame, beat up, murder, or bad-mouth. None of the above is a good idea, even if you really got a bad deal. I've had some real injustices inflicted on me, that cost me thousands of dollars as well as lost prestige, enough to make a full grown man just lay down and bawl. (And mentally at least I probably did that a few times.) But after you have some experience with this situation you know there is really only one good thing to do.

When it happens, calmly ask and make sure you find out exactly why the change in your employment was made. You might not always get the full truth about it, but ask for it, as pleasantly as you can. Understanding the reasons is the only chance you have to fix, change, avoid, or adjust things, either now or in the future. This is beneficial for both parties and it's the first important step toward growth or getting something else. (And you will need something else, for there will surely be a tomorrow, even if it doesn't seem like it right now.) In truth most of us who are terminated deserve it, if we would be honest with ourselves. So discovering and correcting the reason should be our first serious pursuit once we get the notice or the news.

Whatever you do, don't rave and rant and stomp off mad, and don't bad-mouth the

building, we made it even better than best, and we went out the door thanking them for what they'd done for us. And we asked them please to call even if there were just some future crumbs that needed taken care of. No one forgets an ending or leaving attitude, and as we did in the case in question here, you'll end up back in there, later if not sooner.

When you leave, go in a way that's friendly, clean, honest, and helpful. Even if there's never a chance to get your job back, a good reference from a past employer can take you a long way.

company. I'm not interested in hiring anyone who comes to me for a job criticizing the company they just left, and most of my fellow business owners feel the same. "Mad" will do you absolutely no good and has a very good chance of blocking future employment. I know it will be tough to hold your tongue, but do it. You wouldn't believe how many terminations have been reversed when the fired person turned on some intelligence and understanding.

In my cleaning company, for example, we've lost hundred-thousand-dollar accounts where we were doing a good job, but the boss's brother-in-law moved in and needed a job and so he got ours. At first we moaned and groaned and rolled around on the floor and held a "boil the boss in hot stripper solution" meeting... all of that was wasted energy. Then we calmly asked for the reasons why, and made them give them to us them in detail. Then in our remaining thirty days, even though we were on the way out, we went to work. We doubled our efforts in cleaning the

The biggest reason of all to please the boss...

Often you can keep your job even if you depress the boss and the boss depresses you. Most people can struggle along whether they like their job or do it well or not. We can generally get by and get paid (and maybe even get a raise occasionally).

Why then, please the boss? For you, so you can feel good about yourself and grow and love what you do every minute of your life. You spend about a third of your entire life around, in contact with, and under the influence and direction of, a boss or bosses. It's pretty dumb—I mean super dumb—to live this time in a lame, ugly, unhappy way. Because that boss time will spill over to and affect the other two thirds of your life the same way. So learn how to live with and please your boss. It's a key to the kingdom of personal happiness.

10 Fundamental Rules of Success

—Carani N. Rao

10 definite steps and keys for creating your own success story

It is observed that throughout the majority of the classics of self-improvement literature, there are 10 core steps or fundamental rules to achieve success which run as a common thread. The purpose of this book is to share with the readers, these 10 proven rules/principles or keys compiled from the vast ocean of success literature. Some of these essential rules include—(**setting a goal, positive mental attitude and self-confidence, purposeful and burning desire, planning and preparation, resources, inputs, discipline, action, persistence or perseverance, prayer and values.**)

Here success is first defined, then the basic rules involved in achieving success are enumerated and explained with relevant anecdotes and stories. To these 10 fundamental rules, a set of success formulae as well as virtue capsules have also been added in the present book.

Pages: 128 • Price: Rs. 96/-
Postage: Rs. 15/-

How to Motivate Others

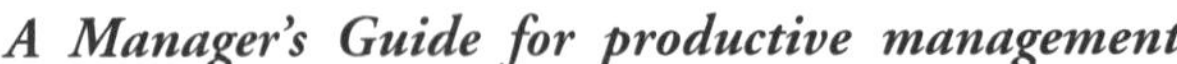

to turn them into super performers

—*Kurt Hanks*

A Manager's Guide for productive management

If you are asked to lead a group or assigned to manage the affairs of an office, you will probably require some tools to succeed. The tool is motivation. Without motivation there is no success. No learning. No action. And, most important of all, without motivation there are no results. This book gives a modern and more effective approach to this age-old problem of lack of motivation. Each page is filled with new ideas, concepts, methods and approach. However, this book is only a tool box—the real solution comes when you effectively match and apply the ideas prescribed to the situation.

The book focuses on:

- The most workable formula for winning people to your way.
- How to move key people from where they are to where you want them to be.
- How to raise other's enthusiasm for your projects.
- What common little quirk causes more problems with others than any other and how you can avoid it.
- What you must see in others, that most people don't see, before you can get them to change.
- Secrets for dealing with stubborn people.
- How to make others take interest in your ideas.
- What everybody wants that you have.
- How to stop others from manipulating you.
- How to criticize without being resented.
- How to give orders that are followed effectively.
- How to get others to like you.
- How to get the ear of the key people in your organisation.

Big Size • Pages: 128
Price: Rs. 96/- • Postage: Rs. 15/-